PART ONE:
THE FIRST FORTY YEARS

POWER
EVANGELIST

TIM HALL

Ark House Press
PO Box 1722, Port Orchard, WA 98366 USA
PO Box 1321, Mona Vale NSW 1660 Australia
PO Box 318 334, West Harbour, Auckland 0661 New Zealand
arkhousepress.com

Cataloguing in Publication Data:
Title: Power Evangelist
ISBN: 9781921589560 (pbk.)
Subjects: Biography
Other Authors/Contributors: Hall, Tim

Front cover design: Anthony Harrison
Layout by initiateagency.com

*I dedicate this book to my wife Jacquelyn,
who is a constant source of encouragement,
and to the many great people of God who
have inspired me to take hold of my destiny.*

TABLE OF CONTENTS

ACKNOWLEDGEMENTS

I began writing this section and it moved, from an acknowledgement, to a chapter, and could easily have become a book. So many wonderful people have had a massive role, both in supporting us and also in the writing of this book. I feared I would miss someone vital and cause grief. I talked with my editor, who suggested it be kept simple. Here then is the very simplified acknowledgement.

I would like to wholeheartedly thank my wife Jacquelyn for pushing me to finish this, our staff for helping me compile it, my editor for getting us to deadline, the people who have financed our ministry over the years, all the family, friends, and ministers who have inspired us, our church for backing us, and especially the One who has made it all possible – King Jesus! Thank you all.

FOREWORD

Tim Hall is one of Australia's great evangelists and has served the Lord faithfully for over 40 years.

After his radical salvation under the ministry of my father, Pastor Andrew Evans, in Klemzig Assembly of God Church, aged 26, Tim Hall felt the undeniable call of God on his life. Filled with the Holy Spirit and a burning passion to do something significant for God, he embarked on a ministry journey that would leave a trail of spiritual 'fire' wherever he went.

Shortly after his salvation, Tim became the Youth Pastor of Klemzig and saw it grow to become the largest youth ministry in Australia. He played a strategic role in the emerging Youth Alive movement, and planted and established a number of significant churches across Victoria, before birthing Tim Hall Ministries and dedicating himself to evangelism across the globe. His crusades are marked by powerful moves of God's Spirit, resulting in mass radical healings, deliverance from bondages, and multitudes of souls swept into the Kingdom.

Tim Hall attributes his success in ministry to a lifetime of relentlessly pursuing the presence of God and the power of the Holy Spirit. Known to regularly retreat to the Australian bush to seek God for days on end, he is unapologetic for urging others to seek God for themselves and do whatever it takes to encounter His power in their life. The resulting spiritual authority is tangible in his ministry and not only draws many to repentance, but also sets people free from oppression.

Tim Hall's life is a testament to what God can do with a broken person who believes by faith that God can use them significantly to build His Kingdom. His story – with its struggles and victories – will inspire you to be all that God has called you to be.

PASTOR RUSSELL EVANS
Senior Pastor and Co-Founder of Planetshakers Church,
Melbourne, Australia
Author of *The Honor Key*

MINISTRY ENDORSEMENTS

Pastor Phil Pringle
Senior Pastor, Christian City Church, Sydney & Founding President Christian City Churches International
"Tim Hall is one of the most unique power ministries we've ever had in our church. Hundreds of lives in our church and thousands of lives throughout Australia and the world have been saved, healed and blessed through Tim's ministry."

Dr. Rodney H-Browne
Senior Pastor/President at The River in Tampa Bay/Revival Ministries International
"I would like to recommend my Dear Friend Evangelist Tim Hall to anyone desiring to have a genuine move of God in their Church. Tim has a great anointing to preach and flow in the supernatural in a unique way. His sense of humor is awesome. He has a heart for souls and I believe your Church would see an increase by having Him minister."

Pastor Brian Houston
Senior Pastor, Hillsong Church, Sydney
"Tim Hall has a passion to see lives changed by the power of the Holy Spirit. He travels throughout Australia and the continents of the globe, with the miraculous power of God transforming lives. Over the years, Tim has been a welcome guest at Hillsong Church, bringing a refreshing touch from God and stirring up our hearts."

Pastor Darlene Zschech
Worship Pastor, Hillsong Church, Sydney & International Artist
"Tim Hall is one of Australia's favorite preachers. He has a unique ability to mix faith with humor to get a congregation hungry and ready for the Holy Ghost to move. Having ministered alongside Tim, I have always seen a move of God take place with many people giving their lives to Jesus Christ."

Pastor Benny Perez
CEO, Pacesetters International & International Evangelist
"The ministry of Tim Hall is a fantastic ministry of authenticity and power. I have personally witnessed Tim as he preaches the Word of God with great anointing and understanding. His ministry is not only marked by proclamation but demonstration of the Spirit of God. Tim is used mightily in signs, wonders and miracles."

Pastor Rick Shelton
Senior Pastor, Life Christian Church, St. Louis
"It is rare that God raises up a ministry that so moves in the power of God and at the same time is so well received across the world. Tim's crusades of tens of thousands have impacted entire nations. When you hear them minister, you will be touched by the power of God and experience the laughter that does good like a medicine (Prov. 17:22). You will never be the same."

Pastor Ray McCauley
Senior Pastor, RHEMA Ministries, South Africa
"Tim Hall is a dynamic faith preaching evangelist who operates powerfully in the areas of soul winning and the moving of the Holy Spirit. He has been a blessing to our church, as he has been to the greater body of Christ for over 25 years. Both Tim & Jacque Hall

will inspire you to hunger after the Spirit of God in great measure and their ministry will lift your faith to a level of expectancy where miracles will take place in your life."

Dr. Andrew Evans
Secretary, world Assemblies of God & Former General Superintendent of the Australian Assemblies of God (1977-1997)

"I have watched the development of Tim's ministry over 25 years and seen God's hand upon him, so that he has become one of the leading evangelists in the world. I have shared with him on a number of occasions in mass crusades in India, Pakistan, and the Philippines during which time we saw thousands of people saved & incredible miracles of healing."

Pastor Frank Bailey
Senior Pastor, Victory Fellowship, New Orleans

"Tim Hall has been my friend and has ministered in our church for several years. He flows in a ministry of signs and wonders, as well as a strong preaching gift. I appreciate his yieldedness to the Holy Spirit and his desire for the Lord to move through him in all of his meetings. Tim has a great love and regard for the local church. I sense his willingness and desire to bless the local church and leave a deposit."

INTRODUCTION

Iwas feeling excited and satisfied as I stepped down from the platform of one of Australia's leading churches some years ago. God had moved powerfully and the atmosphere was still charged.

Waiting for me was a former school teaching colleague from a few years before. He had a big smile on his face, as he strongly declared, "Tim, you inspire me greatly!" I felt excited at his words, which tickled my self-esteem. I should have left it there but, instead, I stepped out and asked, "In what way?" His answer was classic as I look back, although, at the time, it felt somewhat deflating: "You inspire me greatly, Tim, because if God can use you, he can use anyone." This was a powerfully true statement that seems even more poignant today after 40 years of ministry across the nations.

Often, as I stand on platforms looking over seas of faces, I have asked myself how it has all happened. I am writing this book to inspire you to truly know that God loves to pick up ordinary, broken, uncertain people, even misfits, to do significant things for God.

Not that I have yet fulfilled my God-given destiny but, over the past 40 years, I have seen enough amazing things that convince me He is not looking for the 'mighty' or the 'noble' (see 1 Corinthians 1:26-31). God is looking for people with a great spiritual hunger who He is raising to carry a mighty anointing of His power.

This book is written to inspire you to live an amazing life for Jesus. Here is my story so far.

CHAPTER ONE

CHILDHOOD

"The two most important days in your life are the day you are born and the day you find out why" – **Mark Twain**

The weekly half-mile walk up High Street to the Golden Square Methodist Sunday School was always eventful. I would join both Brian and Colin in a walk or feverish sprint to our destination. If we had tormented Ian Miller, the big boy of our street, too severely, we had to sprint like startled gazelles. He was much bigger and stronger than us but we eight-year-olds had great speed. After baiting Ian, the son of a goldminer, we would have to run for our lives yelling and laughing and disturbing the Sabbath rest of the Golden Square locals. A few apples were thrown into the small shop where the strange 'Apostolic' people were worshipping God. This was accompanied by some disturbing animal noises uttered forth as we dashed past their small church. On we ran past the fire station and the monument built on the spot where the gold had first been discovered in Bendigo, Victoria. This discovery had triggered one of the greatest gold rushes in history.

On we dashed, red-faced, puffing, and still taunting our friend Ian whose threats were growing in intensity. On we ran past the Blacksmith's shops, 'Stoona' Woodman's garage, past White's

Bike Shop and the pub and into the safety and security of the Sunday school. We never tired of this adventure. Red-faced, sweaty, puffing and blowing, we joined a large group of young people to be taught God's word.

On the front of the Golden Square Sunday School is its year of foundation, 1852. What an incredible era of action and adventure it must have been at this time in Bendigo, 'The Golden City.' This was a time when intrepid, industrious and fearless men filled with courage and huge vision impacted Australia by a massive molten stream of flowing gold that came from many thousands of mines and the work of a multitude of prospectors in this district. It excites me that my own family played a very significant part in the establishing of the mining industry of Bendigo that impacted Australia in such a huge way. They also amassed large fortunes. My great uncle went on to own and part-own 86 mines. Before looking at some of the daring acts of my forbears my Sunday school needs to be considered.

Here in 1851, on the very spot where the Sunday school stands today, a local preacher from South Australia named James Jeffrey stood on a tree stump in open bush, with tears streaming down his face, earnestly preaching the undiluted Word of God to a crowd of miners, merchants, prospectors, and pioneers. These meetings continued Sunday after Sunday and in 1852 at the cost of £130, of which £50 was collected in one morning, our Sunday school building was erected at the sight of the revival. Mr. Jeffrey continued ministering across the Bendigo mining area with many outdoor campaign meetings. Then log hut buildings for worship were built and many church congregations established. Next to the Sunday school stands the Golden Square Methodist Church. It is a magnificent spired building with large seating capacity, and for me, it is so significant. This church grew out of a genuine revival move that had spread across the Bendigo gold fields.

We were Methodists indeed, tea-totaling, non-drinking, non-smoking, strict observers of the 'Sabbath,' Wesleyan Methodists who never missed church. Everyone dressed in their 'Sunday best' for church and all the ladies wore their hats. Hats were a big deal at that time. Most of the men also wore hats. I think it was a habit established during the war that had only finished a decade previously. It was in this great classical building, with its massive organ and stained glass windows, that I had my first encounter with God. It is strange how memories fade in archival storage units in our mind, yet God encounters are as real as the present moment. They resonate in our spirit with the same life energy of the moment of their occurrence no matter how long ago they have occurred.

I was eight-years-old when God briefly quickened something profound in my spirit. It was the Sunday School Anniversary and we children were sitting in the church in prime position (the choir section) to see a full house of hundreds of people. Looking out over the crowd that day I experienced something profound. As I looked at all the faces I became stirred with the thought that in later days I would somehow be involved with great seas of faces. I felt a divine sense of destiny fill my young innocent heart. I think I knew at that moment the seeds of the call of God. It would be another 18 years until God would cement His call on my life.

I was born on the 16th of December 1948 to great parents. I always like to thank my mother for taking the time to be with me at my birth. I was born by caesarean section after a long and traumatic time that almost cost my dear Mum her life. After 20 hours of labour, forceps, and finally Caesarian section I came into the world. When my Dad first saw me he said I looked like a skinned rabbit. At the time of writing this, my Mum has passed on to be with Jesus at the age of 99 years and 10 months, having come into the world back when World War I commenced.

Mum had already lost my sister Elizabeth some years earlier. She had lived only eight hours. The traumatic birth had resulted in fatal head injuries to Elizabeth. Child bearing had become difficult for my mother as she had fallen 60 feet down a mineshaft when she was much younger. This damaged her pelvis and made it a challenge for her to bring to birth her children naturally. She told the story of how she was taken into Heaven when she delivered me into the world. She had seen green trees and incredibly lush green grass. The peace she felt had put her mind at rest for all these years that there is a Heaven and now she is enjoying that wonderful place.

I am a true 'Baby Boomer.' Dad served with the 2/16th Field Company A.I.F (Australian Infantry Forces) in the Middle East and Papua New Guinea during World War II. He returned from the jungles of New Guinea with malaria, chronic dermatitis and brucellosis, which is a disease normally found in cattle. After an extended period of rehabilitation, he joined the 'topographic' (map-making) unit based at 'Fortuna' in Bendigo.

The walk up Thistle Street from our home next to the Bendigo Creek to the 'Fortuna' mansion took about 25 minutes. It always felt like a real adventure. Dad was the regimental sergeant major at my great uncle's mansion that, since World War 2, had become a military base. I was fascinated watching my Dad working on huge maps spread across large benches. Such a large part of the mapping was done with huge clear rules, squares, and coloured inks. How things have changed with the computer age. It was an exciting place of khaki clad military people. It was just over a decade since the war and many of the soldiers here had fought in the deserts of North Africa and the steamy jungles of Papua New Guinea. There was a great sense of excitement that seemed to fill the air in this new era of expectation. For us young boys 'Fortuna' was like no place on earth. The mansion, with its huge man-made lake and massive areas of trees and foliage, created a limitless adventure environment.

The mansion had first been built in 1855 on the site of the first crushing mills on the Bendigo gold fields. My great uncle George Lansell bought the property in 1871 for £20,000, which would likely equate to several million dollars in today's money. In the ensuing years, George spared no expense in the huge extensions and sheer opulence lavished into every room. Everywhere in the forty-room mansion was lacework, romantic classic facades, statues on parapets and even a huge fountain commissioned as a replica of a huge classic fountain in Pompeii. We would explore every inch of the property including spider-infested tunnels and areas that must have been part of the mining days. As boys the rumour of Uncle George's ghost roaming the property added to the excitement. We would dash through one underground tunnel at full speed trying to avoid an icy hand seizing hold of us.

We spent much of the summer swimming in the lake or catching a few fish. Given the fact that huge amounts of arsenic (associated with gold mining) are still on the property, it›s good that we survived.

'Fortuna' was truly our adventure playground; our very own theme park.

My memories of my Dad meticulously cleaning and polishing his kit ready for parades, the crunch of military boots on the parade ground, and the sight of the lines of men (mostly returned soldiers from World

War II), always sent a thrill of excitement through me. Dad always seemed a man's man to me and I loved him dearly. I have only superb memories of him. In later years, as a 16-year-old boy playing cricket against hardened men, the sight of my Dad standing in the outer caused me to stand up on the inside. His presence stirred the man in me to stand up and face my fears. In the same way, my Heavenly Fathers presence drives fear far from me and causes a standing up on the inside with a boldness that is not my own. I loved my Dad dearly and have only great memories of him. One hour before he left this planet I still recall giving him a huge hug and thanks for being the best father possible. 'Fortuna' was an incredible place to visit, not just because my Dad worked there but because this massive mansion was the personal home of my great uncle George Lansell, known as 'The Quartz King of Australia.'

There is something very sobering and most stimulating in my family's history. So many of my friends call me a 'name dropper'; well, some names are truly worth dropping.

My great grandfather, Wooten Lansell, was an amazing man. He was a real seafarer and adventurer while his brother George was a grocer and tanner. They were from Margate, Kent, England where Wooton was born in 1824. Wooten sailed to many parts of the earth on those wonderful square-rigger sailing ships. He was a real adventurer. Later he would sail on the *Preston Gee Bomagee*, bringing soldiers of the 11th Regiment to old Sydney town. His second trip, as third mate on the *Lord Peter*, brought 300 convicts, soldiers and crew members to Tasmania. In his letters he describes the harsh treatment of convicts and the daily firing of the deck guns to check that all was in order and not tampered with. Numbers of convicts were assigned to work with him and he noted their willing eagerness to work. He was certainly troubled at times by the harsh treatment of the convicts. His next trip was on the *Castle Eden* with 350 convicts. In his journals he describes in detail these amazing journeys.

After four epic trips, which took him from Australia, China, Japan, and Ceylon (Sri Lanka), he came again to Australia on the *Lapwing*, a boat of only 64 tons. It was an incredibly bold thing to bring this tiny vessel such a vast distance through potentially deadly seas. Wooten disembarked from the vessel in Adelaide, South Australia. The *Lapwing* set sail shortly after and was wrecked and lost soon after traveling only 100 miles or so from Adelaide. Wooten became a mounted policeman in the Adelaide Hills then began prospecting for gold near Echunga in the same area. After spending some time in Adelaide, South Australia, he moved across to Victoria to the gold diggings in Bendigo. The year was 1852, which was the same year as the breakout of the Methodist Revival. He was only 28-years-old. I would love to have heard his stories of rounding Cape Horn and the great seas that were confronted. The days of the great tall ships and the courage of exploration fill me with excitement. I know that something of the quest for adventure that inspired Wooten has come flowing down the family tree to me. I have the urge to travel to the nations with the Gospel. Now my son David has been bitten by the same 'bug'.

While living in Bendigo, Wooten discovered enough gold to establish a very successful butchering business. He then sent mail to Margate, England, calling for his brothers George and William to join him. The opportunities and business possibilities excited his brother George particularly and the Lansell brothers began the Australian adventure. They set up a successful business involving butchering, tallow, soap and candle making, and began building considerable wealth.

Wooten, my adventurous great grandfather, married and bought property at Leichardt, near Bendigo, Victoria. I vividly remember visiting the family farmhouse as a young boy. Wooten was highly successful and continued to invest in mining. He also fathered my grandmother Phoebe Lansell who loved me and, I am sure, saw the hand of God on me as a child. As a little boy, I remember what a powerful woman of dynamic faith she was and, I am sure, she prayed often for me to serve and have faith in God. I loved staying at 'Belmont,' the family home named after one of the family's highly successful gold mines. There was a real peace that seemed to surround this amazing lady. Looking back, there was an anointing of the Holy Spirit that radiated from her. 'Belmont' was another magnificent home surrounded by gardens, which seemed to us children of the Hall family like a well-manicured jungle adventure park. The only intimidating part of the lavishly furnished home was the cellar. I don't ever recall going down there. My bedroom in the house was directly opposite the entrance to the cellar. My fertile imagination contemplated the fearsome creatures that made their home in that dark, foreboding place.

Belmont also had a photo of my bearded great grandfather John Hall. His eyes always followed me. They were piercing and could watch me wherever I was in the room.

Uncle George Lansell's statue stands high and tall in High Street Bendigo. 'The Quartz King's' pioneering ventures into quartz reef mining were revolutionary and impacting on a global scale. He revolutionised the whole mining scene in Bendigo, and ultimately owned thirteen major mines was and a large part-owner of seventy-six others. In one two-week period, from the Garden Gully United mine alone, £12,666 were costs while dividends to shareholders was £220,875, distributed over a few months. This was only one mine. One mine he purchased for £30,000 was the 'Pioneer 180.' It was considered to be finished, but upon extending of the very first scope, it yielded £180,000 in a few days. That is $360,000 in our currency today (based on the two for one exchange rate of the 1966 introduction in Australia of decimal currency). By today's standards, at the current gold price, that figure would equate to conservatively 100 times that amount, therefore approximately $36,000,000. That's a pretty decent week's income. The shareholders would have been in orbit. The mind boggles at the wealth coming from his eighty-nine mines. He then directed this mine 'The 180' deeper and deeper to 3.179 feet, the deepest mine in the southern hemisphere at that time. This was global pioneering. It is said that he had some involvement and interest in every quartz gold mine in Victoria, perhaps Australia. His 40-room mansion with a man-made lake was one of Bendigo's significant landmarks and one of my favourite childhood memories.

My other paternal great grandfather John Hall, who was a very committed Christian, came from Durham, England, and also made a vast fortune as an owner and investor in mines. He was a greatly successful businessman. He purchased into mines in Bendigo, Maldon, Ballarat, Rushworth and Gippsland. Besides being a daring investor, the thing I like most about this great grandfather was his strong Christian faith. He was a preacher with a passion to minister the love of Christ to the miners who were enduring great hardship and struggle. Each of these great ancestors was known for their genuine faith in Christ and huge generosity.

My grandfather Thomas Hall, another strong Methodist, was also an investor in mines having received a huge inheritance from John Hall. I was actually named after Thomas and that was quite a story. For some reason, this man (who incidentally was an extraordinary sportsman) was always called 'Tim' or 'Timmo.' I was christened Gordon Stewart Hall in the Methodist church. However, after visiting my Grandad when I was six-weeks-old, my Dad realised that, even though we had several Tom's in the family, we had no Tim's named after Tom. So I got the title 'Tim Hall.' I was never called Gordon. To end the confusion, I added Timothy to my name by deed poll for $2 when I was 27-years-old. I found out after that the name Timothy comes from the Greek *Timotheus*, which means 'One who honours God.' I like to think that God chose this name for me.

My Mum's side of the family is also quite extraordinary. Perhaps the person on her side who most inspires me is my great uncle Major General George James Rankin (DSO and Bar). After an extraordinary military career, he retired from the army as a Major General. He then began a very colourful career as a politician. His fame came from one of Australia's military achievements at Beersheba during World War One in the then Palestine. After enlisting in the 4th Light Horse Battalion George left Rochester Victoria, taking three of his own horses. The 'wailers' were a hardy, powerful Australian breed that had amazing strength and resilience. After time in Egypt the light horsemen, without their horses, were shipped to Gallipoli. There they suffered appalling losses especially at the battle of the Nek. He was wounded but proved to be a most impressive soldier. By 1917 he was a Major and significantly involved in the battles that saw the Ottoman Empire defeated and dismantled. Amazingly, the Australian Light Horsemen, now with their horses, would face and defeat the same Turks that they had faced at Gallipoli. It was here, at the famous charge at Beersheba, that he won his first Distinguished Service Order. The citation for the award makes me immensely proud to be his relative. Here is the wording:

Major George James Rankin,
DSO and Bar, 4th Australian Light Horse Regiment

"As second in Command of the 4th Australian Light Horsemen Regiment, he displayed great gallantry and judgement in the organization of the Regiment during the attack in BEERSHEBA on 31st October, 1917 and the re-organization of the unit and consolidation of the position after the attack. Throughout all the operations he, by his personal bravery, and great coolness, considerably influenced all ranks by the splendid example set by him. Recommended for the DSO."

His second distinguished service order was won at the taking of Damascus. Here is the citation for this medal:

Major George James Rankin,
DSO, 4th Light Horse Regiment

"For great gallantry, dash and initiative during operations, from El Kuneitra to Damascus. On the 30th September 1918, when his regiment acted as advance guard from Sasa to Kaukab, owing to his rapid movements, they captured 340 prisoners, one field gun, and eight machine guns. Kaukab was strongly held by the enemy, and when this officer was ordered to make a frontal attack, his leadership was excellent, and his regiment seized all objectives, capturing nine officers, over 70 other ranks, and eight machine guns. In this action the enemy's cavalry were driven in disorder towards Damascus. On the morning of the 1st October, 1918, when ordered to seize Military Barracks in Damascus, he showed great skill and manoeuvring his troops in such a manner that he was largely instrumental in capturing the whole enemy garrison in Damascus, numbering over 11,000."

Major George James Rankin was a soldier of soldiers. I love to read the description of him as a man of "great gallantry, dash and initiative." I would like to be remembered one day for these qualities. He was described as a man of "personal bravery, and great coolness," and one who "considerably influenced all ranks by his splendid example." What a testimony. I would like to achieve all of these qualities in my ministry for Christ.

These are characteristics that should be woven into our Christian walk. How amazing that he was such a vital part of the taking of the wells of Beersheba in that heroic charge of the Light Horsemen in October 1917. These young Australian men had charged for over a mile of ground, into a hail of machinegun and artillery fire. The famous charge resonates in the hall of valour as 800 men rushed headlong at 5000 entrenched Turkish warriors.

My great uncle played a vital part, not only in making history, but being a significant part of prophecy fulfilled, as the defeat of the Ottoman Empire saw Israel become a nation.

Entering the world in 1948 ensured that my childhood memories are filled with military images. World War II had only recently concluded and the world was entering a whole new phase. Men wore hats everywhere and most smoked 'roll em' cigarettes. Four or five years wearing a slouch hat or helmet, smoking plenty of tobacco established a habit! It was an amazing era of new hope, certainty and family values. Men tipped their hats to ladies as they walked past and people seemed to embrace community values and the loyalty of 'mateship' strongly.

My father and his three brothers had all seen active military service in army and air force. My uncle Wooten (named of course after Wooten Lansell) and my Dad were engineers with 2/16th Field

Company in North Africa and Papua New Guinea. Uncle 'Woot' was quite a character, always seeing a business opportunity and pursuing it with real purpose. Being bombed night after night for many months at Mersamatru, North Africa, gave him the perfect business opportunity. When the bombs rained down on them night after night for seven months and everyone went for cover they would get out of their foxhole and raid the British Officer's supply truck, effectively building a thriving grocery business. One night, Uncle 'Woot' and his 'dugout' mates went out to transact business as usual. On their return, to their stunned amazement, they found an unexploded bomb sticking out of one of the men's bedding. Had he been there, the bomb would have gone through him. Who said, "crime doesn't pay"? I actually believe my grandmother's prayers were powerfully working. While Uncle 'Woot' raided and advanced his business my Dad slept through the bombing raids. No matter how close they came to him, he slept with total peace and security in God. He would get up in the mornings asking what had happened. The only worry or fears he had were for the safety of his brother Woot.

Dad committed his life to Christ under one of the great early preachers who had often come to Bendigo, Victoria. He talked of 'Gypsy' Smith, the great evangelist who had visited Bendigo.

The city of Bendigo has experienced a number of significant revivals over the years. I personally believe that this beautiful city, placed right in the middle of the State of Victoria, has God's hand upon it in a very supernatural way. Even the name is significant. Originally called Sandhurst, it later became Bendigo. Bendigo was named, we understand, after an English Pugilist (Boxer).

"The name of the creek that subsequently gave its name to the goldfield and township is widely believed to derive from an employee of the sheep run who was handy with his fists and nicknamed "Bendigo" after the Nottingham prize-fighter William 'Bendigo' Thompson (his nickname having been corrupted from the biblical 'Abednego')."[1]

An 1878 newspaper called *Australian Town and Country Journal* notes, "Mr. Grice writes: Tell your friends who want to know the origin of Bendigo, that it was named by Tom Myers, Heap and Grice's overseer, in 1841. Tom himself was a bit of a dab with his fists, and a great admirer of the boxer Bendigo: hence the name."[2]

This boxer, one of 21 children, had been named by his mother after Abednego, one of the three boys in the book of Daniel who would not burn in the burning fiery furnace. Obviously his mum's spelling needed some attention. The boxer's claim to fame was his capacity to throw a house brick 70 yards across a river near his home.

"The turning point in Bendigo's life came when he went to a revivalist meeting conducted by Richard Weaver, the ex-collier and evangelist preacher at the Mechanics Institute, Nottingham. 'I was determined to alter the course of my life so I resolved to go and hear him,' Bendigo later recounted. 'And when Mr. Weaver saw me in the body of the hall, he invited me to step on to the platform, which I did, and thank God that I did. For I gave my heart to God and have been a changed man ever since.'"[3]

"Bendigo [Thompson] eventually became a Methodist evangelist, though illiterate he had his own way of delivering a sermon. Adopting a boxer's stance, he would point to the hard-earned trophies by his side and address his audience with the following words: "See them belts, see them cups, I used to fight for those. But now I fight for Christ."[4]

After the war families were especially close, certainly ours was. My praying grandmother had drenched her boys in prayer for safety and she knew how to touch the throne of God. On one occasion, her canaries escaped the cage and she amazingly prayed them back. Canaries unlike pigeons don't come back. I suppose, having read how Moses had split the Red Sea, Joshua had stilled the Sun, and Peter's shadow healed the sick, for my grandmother, canaries returning to their cage, were no challenge. When her four boys came home safely from serious theatres of action during World War II, the family rejoiced greatly and became closer than ever. Dad spent time recovering in Melbourne's Heidelberg Repatriation Hospital, while Uncle 'Woot' was seriously hearing impaired, probably from his grocery business activities, and was pensioned.

Our families were often together and the relationship with all the cousins was very special. I have great memories of shooting rabbits with my cousin Harold at Huntly, or of us shooting 'at' them with the blackwood bow and arrow that Dad had bought back from Papua New Guinea, a place that had won his heart.

He often talked of working with the 2/16th Field Company building a road from Wau near Lae to Bulldog in the Gulf Province. For six months they carved out this road over the massive Owen Stanley Ranges of Papua New Guinea. Much of the work was done with pick and shovel. He described being in wet clothes the entire time. He said the days were steaming hot and humid with perspiration pouring off them as they worked. Then daily the rain bucketed down. The nights on the other hand were so cold that frosts were common. He talked of working on the road when suddenly Japanese aircraft flew past so close that he could see the pilots face. He described the great landslides and the incredible 'Fuzzy Wuzzy Angels' (native Papua New Guinean stretcher bearers) who carried the sick for miles over treacherous terrain to aid stations. He was one of those men.

Dad's talk of Papua New Guinea put a love for that nation in me, which has had a huge impact on my life, as we shall see in the chapters ahead. To this point, I have been involved in 42 campaigns across the nation with tens, or even possibly hundreds of thousands of these dear people making decisions for Christ.

Growing up without television, iPods, X-Boxes, Wii's, iPhones, etcetera, was a blessing indeed. We were outdoor kids. Trees existed for climbing. Old wood and wheels were for building billy carts for the most demanding downhill runs. 'Guy Fawkes Night' (named after the conspirator to blow up British parliament on 5th November 1605) was one of the great events. 'Cracker Night' (fireworks) was a mighty and dangerous event that consumed our minds for weeks. Saving up for huge paper bags of explosives in the form of 'crackers' was essential. All the boys, and a few rugged girls, from our street, built big 'bonnies' (bonfires). Peter Angwin, the tough kid from next door, ruled with an iron fist as, like slaves in Ancient Egypt, we dragged scrub with ropes for miles for wood for the bonfire. It was a huge job as we were not yet ten-years-old. The 'bonnies' grew and were topped with tyres especially from White's bike shop. Guarding the 'bonnies' from other kids was vital, as setting alight someone else's 'bonnie' was fair game. The big night drew together all families of the street plus 'ring-ins'. The lighting ceremony was hushed and solemn then mayhem erupted, always with casualties. If it was not Brian White falling backwards into the Bendigo Creek (an eight-foot fall into concrete) sustaining concussion, or someone getting pushed over into the edge of the fire, it was fireworks injuries. I recall a 'double-banger' being dropped into my back pocket, causing serious trouser damage and buttock burns. But that was in the rules. I can almost smell the gunpowder and see the out of control skyrockets whistling over our heads. The next day we had our debriefing in Brian White's yard under the apple tree. Burns had been treated with some yellow cream from a tube and stories told and retold. We talked as if we had survived some great battle of the ages. Young people today have so many electronic ways to amuse themselves yet often seem bored. We were never bored but always planning some kind of event.

We loved the movies. The Saturday Matinee was an event, costing two pence by tram to the city. I think the movie cost about the same. Jaffas were the 'lolly' (candy) of choice, for rolling down the timber floor with a lovely rattling sound, throwing, or even eating. Comics were swapped at half time (interval), helping to spread chicken pox, mumps or measles across Bendigo. 'Phantom' comics were the premium trading currency. Movies varied slightly. In the 1950's, Westerns dominated week after week, the cowboys and Indians 'whooped' it out, whether in black and white or colour. Alan Ladd was invincible. I still recall the ongoing adventures of 'Captain Video' that always left us desperate to return for the next great instalment. For two pence a big bag of hot chips accompanied us on our two-mile tram ride home.

Amazingly, by the standard of today, it was safe and secure for a group of eight and nine-year-olds to have these adventures without our families being concerned. This was a great life. If we were not climbing the mulberry tree, we were building forts, exploring mine sights, drawing, painting, finding all the mysteries of the great mansion 'Fortuna', swimming, or fishing in its great lake. Life wasn't much different to Mark Twain's story of Tom Sawyer on the Mississippi. We lived outside; our house only existed for eating and sleeping. Relationships with family and friends were close and wonderful but in 1958 it was all about to change for a ten-year-old who loved life in this historic gold mining city.

CHAPTER TWO

ADVENTURES OF YOUTH

"Life is either a great adventure or nothing" – **Helen Keller**

LEAVING BENDIGO- NEW BEGINNINGS IN ADELAIDE- LUCINDALE

I have always had a love of steam locomotives (trains). They always seemed to me, and still do, like great steaming, breathing, living things. As a young boy I would often go to the Bendigo Station with my Dad and stand on the footbridge that crossed the railway tracks waiting for the great steel 'Leviathan' to come steaming and smoking beneath us. Travelling down to Melbourne by train was an adventure for a young boy, especially the tunnel at Big Hill. Bravely, we would put our head out of the window risking a few cinders in the eyes to get a view of the carriages ahead following the great smoking steel machine. How exciting that my Uncle Alf, or Alfred, was a train driver. I am certain that almost every young boy of my era would have wished to sit up in that metal cabin and be a train driver. Yes, my own Uncle Alf sat at the controls of these great engines running between Bendigo and Melbourne.

As a young boy, a friend and I would go through the well-known hole in the fence at the rail yard and sneak down the track to await a

19

major life-impacting event. The steam engines, after returning from Melbourne, would go down to the turntable, which was a massive flat wheel that turned the engine 180 degrees, and faced it back towards Melbourne. The turntable was so huge that the engine and coal truck would move forward onto it and then, with a great strong sound, turn hundreds of tons of steel in the opposite direction.

We would meet Uncle Alf's engine at a set point and hear his booming voice, "Come on up Timmo, and bring your mate." He and his right hand man, the stoker, wore a wonderful uniform of overalls and a hat. They seemed so confident at the controls of the steel monsters. What a job they had! Up the steps we climbed into the cabin. It was a huge, hot, greasy, dirty, smoky, metal filled, intimidating but wonderful environment. There were big metal levers, dials and the blazing fire.

The young people of today can have their X-Boxes and Wii's, I will take the cabin of these steel 'Leviathans.' The excitement in our hearts as we chugged down to the turntable shed was almost unbearable. Sitting up there in the driver's domain made you feel that you were indeed 'the king of the world.' Watching the rotation of the turntable was the pinnacle of the experience. Health and Safety issues were never considered. The word 'sue' in the 1950's only belonged to the girl who lived in your street.

Uncle Alf was one of my true heroes. After all, what better job existed than his? He was also a great cook. When we stayed at his home he would boil the milk for our breakfast cereal and then scrape off the cream, always giving it to me. I have vivid memories of Uncle Alf and Auntie Dorothy's home in Graham Street, Quarry Hill, Bendigo. At night we would sit in the kitchen listening to the radio. We would hang off every word of "The Creaking Door", or listen nervously to

"The Escape of the Amethyst," a naval vessel cautiously finding its way down the Yangtze River, or imagine the saloon scenes in the west as "Trick Mason," the "Gunshot Gambler" dodged hot lead and always survived another torrid gunfight. Uncle Alf was a hero to me, not just because he was a particularly nice man who made us feel important, but because he drove steam trains.

As I arrived at the Bendigo Station on this particular day, although I felt some real excitement, it was clouded by a strange unease and sense of loss. My father's time in the Army had come to an end with his retirement due at 55-years-old. He had sought for work and had been offered a job as a draftsman in the Lands Department in Adelaide, South Australia. It is interesting that we would return to the city where my great grandfather Wooten Lansell had first lived, which set up the incredible years that followed for our family from the mid 1850's.

As our leather cases were placed onto the heavy timber carts that transported our luggage onto the train, we boarded the carriage and my ten-year-old heart was filled with many emotions. Our hand luggage and rugs were placed in the decorative metal racks above our seats and we sat down on high-backed, hard leather, polished, studded seats of our heavily timbered compartment. I sat back and looked at my mother as we waited for the jerk and shudder of the train as we set off into a totally new life. It is now over fifty-seven years since that train jerked and rattled out towards the suburb where I had lived but a few memories are as clear and vivid to me as if it had been yesterday.

In many ways my life had been one that could have fitted into a Mark Twain novel, as we explored mines and lived outdoors as healthy curious young boys. I thought of my grandmother who was so special to me, the closeness of our family and all of my cousins who meant so much to me. I terrorised the girl cousins, annoyed the older male cousins, ruined Christmas family photos by making stupid faces but I dearly loved being with them. I had great uncles and aunties and the bond of the family, probably strengthened by the war years, created something so embracing. What would happen now so far away? We would not be taking the 'rattler' train from Bendigo to Nyah West, near Swan Hill Victoria, again. I so enjoyed those times staying with my grandfather and about 30 cats that lived under the water tank at the home he had built in Nyah West. The rows of vines and the flowing Murray River up there seemed even further away. I had memory flashes of sitting up on the train line with cousins Bill and Julia rolling and smoking great cigarettes using tea and toilet paper. I thought of our trips on sandy tracks out to cousin Charlie's farm at Tooleybuc, not far from Nyah West. When we first went out there the farm had no electricity. Gas lamps still lit the rooms. I still recall my Auntie Alice constantly warning Uncle John, who had major hip problems, not to go in with the pigs. The family were afraid he would fall over and the pigs would eat him. Imagine your Uncle John being eaten by pigs? Life from my earliest memories at around four years until this day in 1958 had been magnificent.

As we boarded the 'Overland Express' for an overnight trip to the 'big' city of Adelaide, I became excited. It had a different sound and feel. It seemed so important, so significant. This was the launch into a brand new day. This trip was very much part of God's great plan for me.

My Dad and our fox terrier dog 'Scamp' were already in Adelaide. There was no time to look back now. Besides, we would be driving back to Bendigo for Christmas in the Hillman Minx. The thought that we would soon be back softened the significance of the move. Adelaide proved to be wonderful. I quickly met a great group of friends one of whom had been intrigued by the new boy named 'Tin Hall.' Yes, they thought it was 'Tin' Hall. Hillcrest Primary School was a good school and my grades were high. We made our first 10-hour Christmas pilgrimage back to Bendigo in the old black Hillman Minx. That was an adventure as it was during the height of summer in Australia and very hot. We drove off at 55 miles per hour for 10 hours in the underpowered, unreliable, English vehicle without air conditioning, totally unsuitable for Australian conditions. Besides that, our dog 'Scamp' always accompanied these trips and due to some digestive problems, continually filled the car with most unsavoury aromas. Mum used wet towels to keep us cool as we didn't even know what air conditioning was. But I loved those early trips to Grandma's place. We broke down several times in places like Lake Cullulleraine or Warracknabeal. The car was old and incredibly unreliable. We broke down at some obscure garage and wondered if we would be there for Christmas. It was exciting and also frustrating.

Adelaide also proved to be a great place to grow up. School was fun. I enjoyed the scouts and I think I had a real zest for life. As a boy I was industrious and soon began to make money as a grocery delivery boy. With a trailer fixed to the back of my bike, groceries were delivered across the suburb. We would ride sometimes more than a mile to deliver one box. This returned a shilling (10 cents). By 12-years-old I was making one pound per week minimum. The average wage in 1960 was around £25, by today's standard my one pound per week would equate to about $40 per week. Not bad money for a 12-year-old.

Life was always exciting because I loved every minute and had a great sense of adventure. I do not remember one moment of ever feeling bored. I still don't. We always carried footballs, often out of shape or with the bladder poking out through the seams, but they were vital and essential to life. The house was where we slept and ate but life was lived outside. Then in 1959 television came to Adelaide. Crowds gathered at electrical retailers to glimpse this marvel of technology. It was not unusual for people to stand with their mouth open in amazement just looking at the test pattern. How good it was when the Jansen family bought one of the first TV's in our street. From memory it was a huge 17-inch screen and black and white of course. It would be placed at the open front window and on hot summer night's families would bring rugs and sit on their lawn watching the old black and white programs. Then the Sharp family bought theirs and we watched all the old shows. Robert Stack bought the 'Untouchables' to us, Elliot Ness was so cool as he confronted Frank Nitti and the Chicago mobsters. Jackie Gleason introduced 'Crazy Guggenheim.' 'Maverick,' 'The Rifleman,' 'Bat Masterson' and 'Paladin' in 'Have Gun – Will Travel' were great. 'Cheyenne Bodie' from the show 'Cheyenne' was my favourite and Disneyland filled our minds with things that we could only dream about. Lucille Ball's voice reminded us of fingernails on a blackboard yet we laughed heartily. Fred Flintstone's "Yabba-Dabba-Doo" came into our lives and we felt for Wilma. 'Sing along with Mitch' was an incredibly popular family programme and was an early form of karaoke. The family would sing along to a range of old and new songs. We "followed the bouncing ball" over the words melodiously beating out to the songs.

Television had come and some people even had coloured filters over the old oval shaped 17-inch screens that gave a hint of colour. We all inwardly wondered where technology possibly could take us now. Television provided for me a programme that gave me so much satisfaction. Personally, I do not think programs on TV can ever attain to the lofty heights provided by 'Curly, Larry and Mo.' Any 'Three Stooges' fans could make all the sound effects, mimic Curly's running with one leg stationary. It was all eye-gouging, heads in vices, hair pulled out by chunks and total insanity. Curly could gnash his teeth metallically and many wondered if Mo might have actually been Adolf Hitler. Years later I showed my children some of the 'Three Stooges' programs and they looked at me like I was strange for finding them funny. I just know that we baby boomers enjoyed slapstick humour. We understood and embraced the uncomplicated lunacy of these programs made in the 1940's.

Life is always exciting for a young boy with a sense of adventure and a love for life. School was wonderful, friends plentiful, and most of our spare time was spent outside playing sport and getting into moderate mischief. Living in a district where the houses had tin roofs was a bonus. 'Roof bricking' nights were thrilling as we pelted handfuls of blue metal stones onto selected roofs. A broadside by six or eight naughty boys on one roof was like an explosion. To get home after a night of mayhem launched on several dozen homes was a challenge. Men with torches roamed the streets to look for us and, with cars driving up and down the road, we had to duck and hide all the way back to our base. The 'Threepenny Bunger Firecrackers' were like a small stick of dynamite, which could blow a tin letterbox 30 feet from the fence. This sport of 'letterboxing' was very popular when we were about 12 or 13-years-old and we were skilled at it. I have since repented of the many letterboxes that we blew apart. I actually feel a bit convicted as I write about it especially, when in a rush of excitement, I blew our own letterbox to pieces.

As I shared earlier, we were a solid Methodist family that attended church regularly. Despite this regular attendance over many years, I had not really heard the Gospel preached in a way that caused me to respond for Christ. I did however have a God-awareness. Attending a Baptist Camp at around 15 or 16-years-old, I made a step forward for Jesus but never really went on in faith nor really knew how to progress. Australian Rules football, cricket and girls took the centre stage, dominating my time for the next few years.

At primary school I had been at the top of the class and gained the offer of a full scholarship to a top private college in Adelaide. I was also invited to sit an entrance exam with students from primary schools across Adelaide who had finished in the top two positions for their final results. From 200 students examined, only 70 would be invited to go on to Adelaide Technical High School, which was an academic arm of the 'School of Mines' in South Australia. I was accepted and began five years that I totally wasted academically. School was fun but sadly football and cricket were about the only things I took seriously. I look back with a sense of shame that I did not use those years to lay a platform for the future. I remember clowning around and helping create situations that stifled learning even for the rest of the class. We learned how to leave sulphur chips and hydrochloric acid in inkwells just prior to the next class coming into the room. It was always with mirth that we watched classes evacuate after us as the pungent stench of 'rotten egg gas' (hydrogen sulphide) engulfed the room. I have since learned that hydrogen sulphide is a highly toxic gas. School life was one huge irresponsible time of great friendship, hilarious stories, which I probably should repent of, academic slothfulness, stringent discipline and commitment to sport. I have never been to a school reunion because those years carry little that I am proud of. I have kept football photos of the fourth year when we won the premiership in our "A" grade division. I remember sitting in Ancient History lessons being totally disinterested and disruptive. Today, I am a fanatical historian with a passion to understand strategies and general-ship in war through the ages. I have walked battlefields of the South Pacific, Gallipoli (Turkey) and parts of Europe, have sat with veterans of the Guadalcanal Campaign of World War II, walked battlefields of the Boer War in South Africa, and studied in depth the campaigns of Alexander the Great, Hannibal of Carthage and others. It would have been wonderful to gain a foundation back there. However, God is gracious and miraculously as I further found myself accepted to study to be an art teacher after my final year of school.

WELCOME TO THE 1960'S REVOLUTION

In my late teens I began tertiary study in the tumultuous late 1960's. The airwaves were filled with the message of a New Age, an age of enlightenment, psychedelic imagery, 'free love', protest songs and revolution. The Beatles took us from 'Love Me Do,' to the 'Glass Onion' and 'I am the Walrus.' The Beatles, Rolling Stones and Marianne Faithful had visited the Maharishi Mahesh Yogi, and George Harrison, who now embraced the Hare Krishna movement, sang 'My Sweet Lord' to Krishna. It was now into this environment that this good Methodist boy, confused, battling with the conflicts of Christian values, and this whole 'New Age of Aquarius', enrolled in the South Australian School of Art to be trained as an art teacher.

Marijuana was plentiful, Vietnam was raging, 'free love' and 'hippies' abounded, 'Pop Art' expressed the materialistic consumerism of the age. *Time magazine April 8, 1966 rhetorically asked the question on its cover, "Is God Dead?" The cover article was in part a reference to the Friedrich Nietzsche quote from his 1882 book The Gay Science, "God is dead."*[5]

The Rolling Stones were looking for 'Satisfaction,' the universities pumped out humanistic, socialist philosophy and everything seemed wonderfully crazy. Psychedelic posters covered our walls and, as youth, we pushed through the stoned haze to find the reality of just who we were. John Lennon declared the Beatles "more popular than Jesus." Despite the horror people expressed, it was possible, for a very short period, to have been true. Andy Warhol pushed the boundaries of gender with the 'Velvet Underground Movement,' while David Bowie, Jimi Hendrix and others questioned all aspects of life, as we had known it. Woodstock had been the opening of another great 'Pandora's Box' as hundreds of thousands of young people in America stayed in mud and rain to listen to the new 'prophets' who pushed a day of awakening, drugs, free sex and "a stand against the establishment." The age of innocence for the youth of planet Earth was over. Everything changed as we entered what was known as the dawning of the 'Age of Aquarius.'

By the end of my tertiary training, painting had become my passion. Large and bright, soul-searching, abstract murals became my quest. Vibrant colour and explosive forms that flowed like lava seemed to express something from deep within that I could not verbalize. I had become an agnostic, believed in reincarnation, UFO's and embraced a hedonistic lifestyle. Tequila was my drink of choice as I drenched my soul with alcohol. Everything seemed to move so fast. A man even walked on the moon. Flags were burnt on college campuses in the USA in protest at the war in Vietnam. In Australia we had joined their President Lyndon B. Johnson, and we were truly going "All the way with LBJ." Conscription had come and our names were in the ballot.

I had no real political or moral views on the War in Vietnam and was open to the possibility and call up of military service in a country that until then was unknown to us. I missed the ballot by one day. They drew the odd numbers for the month of December and, as my birthday is the 16th of December, I missed the call. In some ways I felt a little disappointed, but in the following days I watched the emotionally fragmented lives of numbers of young men upon their return from the Vietnam conflict and was glad I missed it. We sent the boys over into the steamy jungles to fight an impossible war, undermined by the media. Then people, who called themselves Australians, pelted them with paint and eggs and shouted 'baby killers' as they returned. How insane it had all became. The war began to polarize Australians and brought with it an unrest never seen before in our great land.

The time I spent studying art in the late 1960's was quite surreal in many ways. It was such a 'brave new world' era and we art students saw ourselves as 'new prophets' in paint, clay and steel. Our philosophy of life was constantly challenged. A whole wave of revolutionary new thinking swept the world's youth. Drugs had opened a totally new sphere of thinking and musicians truly became the 'Aquarian evangelists.' I use the word carefully, as it was not 'good news' they brought. Certainly, we saw ourselves as a mouthpiece to a generation that in one decade lost their innocence. It was now a "walk on the wild side."

I finished my training with a deep appreciation of art and a desire to produce my own bright, swirling, colour-charged canvases that would impact those who viewed them. I had made some great friendships and we would talk for hours about using colour and form to express our persuasion for life. Our minds had been filled with multiplied images of Andy Warhol, the iconic comic images of Roy Lichtenstein, the experimental and intellectual Art of Victor Vasarely, which was so complex visually that it would cause your head to spin. We had studied the Dadaist and Surrealists who had pushed us to explore the regions of the unconscious and dream-like images that confounded the intellect. The haunting metaphysical landscapes of Giorgio de Chirico fascinated us and we were inspired by the massive paint dribbled canvasses of Jackson Pollock. 'Blue Poles' by Jackson Pollock was purchased by the National Gallery of Australia in 1973 for a huge price ($1.3 million). "Anyone could paint that," was the view of so many Australians who were disgusted that tax money could be wasted on 'rubbish' but I personally have always enjoyed Pollock's work.

I turned 21-years-old and headed into all the excitement that life could offer. I finished three wonderful, colourful, mind-stretching, and somewhat confusing yet satisfying years of tertiary study. I emerged with a Diploma of Teaching, and a passion to paint having earned a high credit grade for painting. I also left the School of Art with deep spiritual uncertainty. It was exciting to receive a teaching posting to a lovely place called Lucindale in the South East of South Australia. The next three years would be pivotal in my spiritual journey.

LIFE IN THE BUSH

School teaching in a country region is a truly great experience. Because I was a fairy handy Australian Rules footballer and cricketer, I received a very warm welcome into the district. I went to live in a farm property about 25 miles from the town on the end of the bus run. I was also a school bus driver. I moved into the shearer's quarters on a beautiful property on the Coles-Spence Road between Penola and Lucindale with a delightful family. It all began so well. The school was progressive. I had my own art room that was well equipped and the staff embraced me. Little did I realise that, with all of the new optimism and the excitement that this new adventure brought, within three years I would find myself in a very dark place both spiritually and emotionally.

Here in Lucindale I had some real success and was recommended for the position of Senior Master (Head of an Art Department) after three years of teaching. I also had some huge failures, made serious errors of judgment and fortunately met wonderful people who taught me the nobility of hard work and inspired me to push through barriers of exhaustion and pain. Here I learned to work hard, drink heavily (self-learned), cart hay, crutch sheep, ride a horse (badly), and became part of a very tight-knit community.

The teaching staff at Lucindale were a joy to work with and the farming families treated me extremely well, even as things turned dark in the days that followed. In life we meet some interesting people who help to shape our lives. It was there that I had the privilege of becoming close friends with Laurie 'Zoomer' Polomka. We met through football, worked together, spent plenty of time in each other's company and got into plenty of trouble. 'Zoomer' was the hardest working man I had ever met and one of the toughest. Playing football, he was fearless. He used his head as a battering ram against knees and boots. When I went to work for him during the school holidays and later during time off from teaching, his work ethic was so inspirational. He taught me the thrill of hard physical work and showed me how to push through even when your body is screaming for mercy.

Carting hay with 'Zoomer' Polomka was magnificent. 'Zoomer' did not get the nickname lightly. He was fearless in life and worked like three men. Carting 80-pound (36-kilogram) bales of hay from 7am to 7pm in 110-degrees (Fahrenheit) heat (43 degrees Celcius), 6 days per week certainly finds something deep and satisfying in a 'city boy.'

Then to be accepted and respected by the locals injected some deep resilience into my life that has helped to push me on when in ministry I have felt totally exhausted.

The farm and country life was wonderful but it was here in Lucindale that I ventured into dark spiritual things that would impact my direction of life significantly. Days and years in the Methodist Church laid a foundation of godliness for me, but throughout that time God and I had still not really met. Church had not filled the great gap in my soul. I later came to realise that only Jesus can fill that gap. Alcohol will not, nor drugs, nor illicit sex, only the flooding reality of Him "by whom the world was created," as it says in the Gospel of John 1:3. It seems that every person has within them a God-shaped vacuum that only God Himself can truly fill.

The art world can be "a strange brew," in the words of the 1967 song by U.K. band Cream. It is so often an intense search into the deep chasms of the human soul. Often that search will take a person on a journey that will be dark and perilous, that is how it was for me anyway. The scary thing is that it typically comes with deep self-searching so often ending with depression and tragic results.

FREEMASONRY

I had become a Freemason and gone through the first three degrees very rapidly. I had sworn some serious oaths and tried to find life's meaning in the Masonic Temple. It is not there. Despite some good friendships formed with men that I respected and a sense of belonging, I felt no spiritual satisfaction or reality in the Lodge. Although at the time fascinating it was still void of spiritual life. I realized after my conversion to Christ that it is no place for a born again Christian.

As an artist, huge impacting canvasses of vibrant forceful colour were my medium of expression. The question often came to my mind, "Can we capture the spirits of the geniuses of art and music that float in the great universal cosmos and draw them into our lives to impact and increase our creativity? Could we find the spirit of Beethoven or Paul Gaugin, Toulouse Lautrec, or even Van Gogh?" This is called necromancy or consultation with the dead (see Leviticus 19: 31 or Deuteronomy 18: 9-12). I wanted to draw creativity from them so I visited 'haunted' places, reached out to the spirit world and became totally entangled. It was into the taboo realm of darkness that curiosity took me. My deep spiritual hunger had never been met in 28 years attending church. How tragic. Many long discussions at art school had whet my appetite for spiritual enlightenment. I was searching for something that would satisfy and answer this inner gnawing and sense of need for some supernatural reality. I was a candidate for deep spiritual deception.

One afternoon a member of our school staff approached me with a big challenge. Something cold and sinister would enter the shearer's quarters where he lived. This self-contained flat was separate from the main house on a large sheep property. He explained to me how his television and lights would turn on by themselves, doors would mysteriously open and at night a dark unseen force would visit the place. He told me he called it 'Casper' in the hope that it would be friendly. My curiosity got the better of me and I had to go and experience this for myself. According to the words of the 'wise' man, curiosity was not a positive thing for 'the cat.' My curiosity and interest in the paranormal led me on a very shaky and terrifying path. I had to know what he was experiencing so I arranged to come out to his place to try to help him explain these phenomena.

The drive to my friend's quarters was around 30 kilometres through the rich and wonderful South Eastern region of South Australia. It is an area of beautiful properties that are heavily timbered with an abundance of rain. It can get quite swampy in areas during winter. My drive that night was on a dirt road, lined with iconic Australian gum trees, ponds and creeks full of water after the heavy rains. At night it could be quite eerie along some sections of road. It was a dark night, cold and windless, as I drove and a strange feeling came over me. It was a mix of real curiosity, unease and some cynicism. I knew my friend was genuinely anxious and afraid of something that he could not explain.

Arriving at his quarters it all seemed quite normal. His place was warm and cosy as we sat down with a few drinks to play a game of chess. Everything was relaxed as we chatted and laughed despite a sense of expectation that something could happen on that cold winter's night. For an hour or so all was normal until everything changed. Suddenly the door opened and slammed shut and the room went noticeably cold. The hair rose on my neck as an unseen entity filled that room. This was real. It was not mind over matter or imagination. I could not move and could hardly even breathe. This unseen thing seemed to be all over me like a blanket. It felt threatening and sinister. I looked at my friend and watched the colour drain from his face as I am sure it had drained from mine also. I was filled with dread and fear knowing that this supernatural force was likely a demon from hell. For what seemed like an eternity the presence hung over us like a canopy. The door slammed again and it was all over. That was horrendous but the thought of a 30-kilometre drive back to the caravan that was my home was nightmarish. I had a number of stiff drinks before driving my Datsun 1600, like Jehu of Old (see 2 Kings 9: 20), back home to my caravan. I had been thrown off the previous property for laying some well-directed blows on the landlord's son. The caravan was my new home down at the Cook's farm. The drive home was fast and I was still shaking from the terrifying encounter I had experienced. My friend explained to me that I had experienced 'Casper'. It seemed that something took place that night that opened some dark gateway into my life.

From that time on I seemed to be constantly aware of unseen powers and presences. Often I would wake in the night standing on my bed ripping things off the walls and shrieking like a scene from some horror movie. Fear and excessive use of alcohol began to build a stronghold in my life. It was not a natural fear that gripped me but a constant sense of an unknown force that it seemed had been sent to destroy me. I would see spiritual things and feel hands on my throat and body during night, undoubtedly knowing that a dark kingdom truly did exist.

I had several serious road accidents shortly after. On one drunken night I lost control of my car at 120 km/h. Hitting water on a dirt road I aquaplaned across a swamp missing trees and large rocks. I sat in a car filling with cold water. I scrambled out through the window and realised that I could so easily have died that night in the icy waters of that swamp. I felt vulnerable and very aware of impending trouble, yet I went deeper and deeper down this dangerous path.

Alcohol took a large hold of me in a way very unlike my Dad, who never in 87 years touched a drop. He always said, "Son, if you want to keep out of trouble, keep out of the pub." I made up for it in a big way. After further road accidents, heavy drinking and crazy living, I knew I desperately needed a new start. I had built a reputation in the district of being quite wild. No one would have been surprised if I had become a road statistic. Many nights of drinking heavily and high-speed driving has claimed so many young lives. I miraculously got out of several wrecks with only stitches, bruises and concussions.

I could so easily have died in a mass of twisted steel on some lonely road or highway. It is sobering to look back on those years and realize just how close to Hell's gates I had been living.

Respect and close relationships in the district had been seriously undermined as I became quite unpredictable. After beating up their eldest son, I had been put off the farm of one great family with the words, "For two years you have been nothing but a bad influence on my children." I was in desperate need of a big life change. I thought it was a change of environment but God had planned a much bigger change, an eternal encounter with Jesus and a mighty infilling and empowering with the Holy Ghost. This was indeed coming, but there was still a walk into darkness that led to a head-on encounter with the Saviour.

CHAPTER THREE

CALLED OF GOD
≫≫≫✕≪≪≪

"For ye see your calling, brethren, how that not many wise
men after the flesh, not many mighty, not many noble, are
called: But God hath chosen the foolish things of the world
to confound the wise; and God hath chosen the weak things
of the world to confound the things which are mighty"
– 1 Corinthians 1:26-27 KJV

REALITY BITES - A NEW LIFE

It is a frightening thing to feel yourself going deeper and deeper into darkness with a sense gripping you that it is a one-way ride. After a night of drinking homemade wine, several Lucindale school staff had tried to take my car keys so that I would not drive back to the farm blind drunk. I became quite violent and later realised I was losing control totally. On so many nights I had slept in my car in driveways of properties, under trees, or even woke up in towns and cities with no idea where I was. I had to have a change of location. God knew that what I needed was not a change of location but a change of Kingdoms. My life was being impacted greatly by forces outside of my control.

Strangely, when I was drunk, I would wander into the backyard, look up into the sky and talk to God. It is amazing that He was working with me, even when I was His enemy. In Ephesians 2:12 we read that without Jesus we were "aliens from the covenants of promise, having no hope and without God in the world." What a tragic place to be. That place is the domain of vast uncountable multitudes today across the earth. Yet God watched and waited for me.

Despite loving my time in the country, it seemed that I needed a new start at a city school. It all sounded like wisdom to me. A large city high school opened its doors to me and I took up residence in a flat near my parents' home. It is good to have your independence and still be able to drop in for Mum's cooking or drop off your washing, knowing that she was so skilled in these areas.

Most of that next year was a blur of parties, heavy drinking, and abstract paintings. I enjoyed teaching, but was rarely in much of a state to do as well as I should have. It was amazing that after only three years at Lucindale with my bizarre behaviour, I was recommended for a Senior Master position. I was a creative teacher and had a gift from God, which enabled me to bring the natural ability out of the students.

It was a confused, somewhat eerie time of massive self-doubt and superstition for me. The spirit realm was intense and foreboding but extraordinary things were coming. Watching a movie called 'Young Winston,' the story of Winston Churchill, I heard a line that went something like this, "I am 26-years-old and have had no adventure". My mind lit up like a bulb you see in the cartoons, as I thought, "Adventure is the answer, a serious and daring adventure". So a four-and-a-half-month trip through Africa to cross the continent sounded logical. An application for a year's leave of absence without pay from the Education Department was obviously the way to go. The application was accepted and the safari planned with a Trans African Safari Group. I thought that this would be the answer. I would take a leave of absence from teaching for a year, go back into the bush for work and do some builder's labouring in Adelaide. I would then fly to Africa and experience a real adventure. This would be the key to a second new start.

I thought of the African safari ahead and all the possible risks and dangers. I thought of lions and African snakes without realising at the time that one of the most 'dangerous' things on planet Earth is a small, older, Spirit-filled, fired up woman of God. When these women of God have you in the crosshairs of prayer, with laser-like purpose, there is no escape. Mrs. McCormack was a radiant saint of God from Northern Ireland whose prayer life was renowned. My dear Mum introduced me to her and also to her boarder Pastor Paul Newsham, who informs me that never a day passed that she did not cry out for me to be saved. Students from my school also began to seek God for my salvation. Numbers of folk from the old Methodist church were fervently praying. The writing was on the wall was for me.

Life continued as a meaningless series of drunken events, friends, sport, and painting. I had no shortage of friends and we lived life following and being conformed to the world's ways. Peer pressure is still one of the deadliest forces on earth. My flat was a bohemian artist's haven with big, bright, abstract paintings hung around the walls, empty bottles, broken-up furniture, a big royal navy flag and a constant flow of friends and acquaintances. But something was changing rapidly, it felt like being in a dark tunnel with a train coming and nowhere to hide. Mrs. McCormack was passionate in prayer and gripping hold of God for me like a bull terrier. Things happen very suddenly when God responds to people's intense prayer. The light in that dark tunnel was not a train but the approaching encounter with the God of eternity.

THE DIE IS CAST

One night an old friend arrived at my flat. His marriage was broken and he had nowhere to live. I had a spare room where I kept my art equipment and miscellaneous goods. We moved a few things around and he was now my flatmate. He was one of the funniest people I have ever met. On Sunday mornings at 5.00 am we would turn the stereo up to full volume and play a variety of bizarre sound effects to the community. The echoes around the block of flats meant no one knew where the noise was coming from. Air raid sirens, police and ambulance sirens, dive-bombers and a range of weaponry would bring everyone out of the flats complaining vehemently. We stood out on the balcony complaining noisily, waving our arms around, and remonstrating. We told everyone from the block of flats that we would find the culprits and deal with them. The air raid siren was so loud it must have woken people for many blocks. I have since repented of those days but still struggle to stifle my grin when thinking about some of the crazy things we did.

His full gorilla suit was a big hit far and wide. Life was a mad time of crazy slapstick humour, chasing girls, heavy drinking and deep depression. Clowns are often the saddest people. He was devastated over his marriage break-up, drank heavily and had struggles with 'astral travel' (out of the body) experiences that he was unable to control.

I came home to my apartment one night to be confronted by a most alarming situation. In a drunken state, he had taken a seven-inch bowie knife, and carved deeply into his own face and arm. He lay on the floor drunk and bleeding. I felt stone cold as a chill went through me. The hair on my neck stood up. Reality struck home suddenly and with force. After he was patched up, I went into my room, shut the door, and tried to calculate where my life was really heading.

At that point an inner voice spoke to me, "Tim, you are on a slippery slide that is taking you and your friends to Hell. If you do not get off it now there will be no return". I shook and perspired as I sought for an old picture Bible that was somewhere in my room. The cry in my heart was like Jonah who cried out from the belly of the whale. The sudden reality that you are actually only one heartbeat from Hell itself can be very sobering. Mrs McCormack and those students were touching Heaven as part of a plan that was established from before the foundations of the earth. It was Jonah who described my action that night as I clutched that old bible.

"Out of the belly of Hell I cried out and You heard my voice." (Jonah 2:2)

I cried out to God for mercy and He truly answered me. I was not truly saved yet or really understood too much about God but something had taken place. This was my first big step forward. Sadly, the drinking and crazy living continued although with less purpose as conviction was setting in.

One day I was unable to attend school because of some alcohol poisoning. I vomited bile and blood and felt very sorry for myself. There was a knock at the door and one of the teachers stood there. Con was a godly man whom I respected. He lived well, spoke extremely well of people, treated me with a respect that I did not deserve, and led the Christian group at school. He bought me a large bag of peanuts, which is still a mystery. "You are in trouble Tim aren't you?" he said with a knowing smile and look of concern. He suggested that I should come and live in their home and that they had set up a painting studio facility for my art. These dear folk were Spirit-filled, Charismatic Anglicans. They were wonderful sincere Christian people. They talked about 'renewal,' and prayed over meals as though God was actually in the room. The scary thing for me was the peace and tranquillity within their home as the presence of God filled each room. They were magnificent people. Their hospitality and warmth affected me greatly and I felt obliged one night to go to their 'Charismatic' Church fellowship meeting. It was a group of Anglicans and Methodists and 'ring-ins' like myself.

What a nerve-wracking experience to hear strange but rather beautiful unknown heavenly languages being spoken. I was fascinated by the way the Anglicans could speak the word 'holy' in such a biblical way. An Anglican Minister received prayer to receive the Baptism in the Holy Spirit. To my amazement, he fell prostrate under God's power. I sat back in the corner and felt quite stunned but aware that supernatural things were happening in that room. Despite some slight hesitation I knew it felt right, unlike the hellish things I had experienced in past years. The suppers at that group were the real draw card with seafood dishes of prawns, oysters and tasty snacks. They were obviously not Jewish. These suppers had an impact as I kept returning.

I went back a number of times but felt that, being a 'good' Methodist boy, a Methodist church was the place I should find God. Several visits to such a church were very difficult. No one approached me nor made me feel welcome. I think people could feel my hedonistic spirit.

Maybe it was the big 'mullet' hairstyle and wild appearance that kept them at bay. I did however keep coming back. Finally, I concluded that if no one spoke to me I would go back to the 'pub' for fellowship. That's why most people go to the hotel or bar. It's for acceptance and company and a feeling of belonging. They put most churches to shame in that regard. People must feel welcome and loved in churches.

Driving up King William Street, the main street of Adelaide CBD, on my way to the church one night I saw a large fluorescent sign on the side of a movie theatre. The sign was very much in the 1960's and 1970's poster style. It had a touch of Hendrix, the Doors and Led Zeppelin about it. The 'Jesus Revolution' sign hung in front of the movie theatre and called me in. I parked the car and entered the theatre. I love old movie theatres. From boyhood I enjoyed the carpeted stairs and the particular smell that filled the atmosphere of these grand old buildings. This was a very different experience. On entering I was overwhelmed by an awesome sense of a strong supernatural presence that both inspired and intimidated me. That's the greatest thing a church can have, a powerful gripping sense of God's tangible presence. These people seemed to be filled with God. A man named Hans, now a Senior Pastor of a church in the Adelaide Hills, met me at the door. He was a big warm-hearted man with piercing eyes and a strong sense of authority. He spoke inspiring and welcoming words and then ushered me through the foyer into the theatre. As I walked in, I experienced an atmosphere that was alive with God's tangible and living presence. Naturally, as a 'heathen', I turned for the safety of the back row, which was truly a dangerous move as there is no safety there. The Mrs. McCormack's of this world target that row in prayer for the naughty young people that choose to sit there. I sheepishly stepped into my seat next to a tall man with an arm similar in size to a man's leg. I remember vividly how he draped this great arm over my shoulder whispering, "God bless you, young man." I think my reply was, "It's cool, I'll be good".

The night was quite overwhelming. The singing, friendly people and powerful 'electric' energy that filled the atmosphere amazed me. As I walked out, Hans greeted me again. His smile and warm attitude has stayed with me all these years. "God has a great plan for your life, my friend. He loves you", were his words as I walked from the theatre. "What just happened tonight?" I asked myself. Something had happened in a process that God was unfolding.

That week I visited my parents. Mum surprised me when she told me that she had heard I was getting 'religious'. She suggested that a mile down the road was a large church with many young people and buses. The 'bus' thing fascinated me and a decision was made to visit this church on the following Sunday.

I asked Con about the credibility of this church with the buses and, after I gained his approval, this seemed the direction to take. From memory, the previous night I had drank solidly and likely had a significant 'hangover,' but Sunday night came and at 5.45pm I walked into Klemzig Assembly of God in Adelaide, South Australia. John De Wolfe, a wonderful Christian man from my old Methodist Church (also a close friend of Mrs. McCormack), immediately greeted me. John's eyes widened with amazement as he saw the young man for whom they had been interceding. I had been targeted in prayer by a group of prayer warriors for some time. John warmly invited me to join them, which seemed positive until I saw scores of students from the school where I taught. I had the reputation of being a drunken, bohemian, psychotic art teacher. I had built this crazy reputation and I suppose I was embarrassed to be seen in church. My first thought was to quickly leave the building but fortunately made the decision to stay at church but in a less conspicuous part of the room. I thanked John for his warm invitation to join his family and then made my way to the farthest back corner of the balcony. I didn't realise but I had chosen to sit in the most 'deadly' place in church that a 'sinner' can choose.

The singing was enjoyable with some of the old classic Pentecostal songs accompanied by a troop of tambourine players. They seemed to raise their streamer-laden tambourines in a nice synchronised way. I seem to recall that "He brought me out of the miry clay" was a favourite. Stepping out of the miry clay and having our "feet on solid rock to stay" did not make too much sense but I enjoyed the enthusiasm and warmth of the song service. Sadly, the preacher 'messed it up' for me. It was Pastor Andrew Evans whose preaching seemed to hold that congregation of 800 or so people in the palm of his hand. He was warm and kind and prone to become emotional as he talked of his Saviour. Tears would flow freely down his face as he described or talked of Jesus. This was fine but at different points in the sermon he would strongly warn and challenge us regarding the state of our souls each time looking directly at me. He seemed to have me in his sights. What had I done? Who had told him that a 'sinner' was up in the balcony? My hands became wet and I kept swallowing hard. By the time he concluded I was shaking, swallowing hard with sweaty palms, and wanting to escape. Yet truly the moment of truth had come. God was about to claim His rightful place as Lord of my life, taking me into this amazing thrilling life that has since been mine for over four decades now. On and on he preached and often gazed my way with seemingly fixed attention.

Now came the ultimatum. The preacher was bringing his message to crunch time. "Who tonight would like to know that every sin you have ever committed is gone, and that Jesus, the Son of God, has come into your life? Lift up your hand if you would like to know Jesus tonight", he declared with authority. "I would like to", I thought, "But I don't particularly like you, preacher". People began to raise their hands. I thought I would wait until he looked away then I would lift mine. As he walked away from my direction, I shot my hand up and down with lightning speed. Amazingly, in a flash, he spotted my gesture. It was as though he had eyes in the back of his head. "I see your hand, that young man in the back row," he said. I was stunned. In addition to the shaking and sweaty palms and my great desire to escape, I was now stunned by this preacher's eagle eye.

Pastor Andrew gave the call for those who had raised their hand to join him at the front of the stage. There was no chance of this happening. There were too many of my school students present. This was too much and my excuses were many. What should I do? People began walking down the aisles, evidently strongly touched by God's word and power. I stood rooted to the spot in the back row and pondered this huge decision. I was going nowhere until, suddenly, God took the next step.

I was in the very back row at the extreme end of the balcony. There was no one behind me. How terrifying it was when I felt an unseen hand placed on my shoulder. The power of God came on me in a way that left me breathless. Now I started walking. It was as though my legs had taken over and I had no choice but to go with them. As I walked down to the front of that church I felt strongholds breaking in my life. Things seemed to be physically lifting off me. I'm sure demons, which I had picked up over the years, were losing their hold as I walked towards Jesus.

It is hard to piece everything together from that point. It is something of a blur. Pastor Andrew, my great friend and father in the faith, tells me that he became confused by a large number of young students, mainly girls, from our school who cried, pointed and gathered around me. God had spoken to him a week or so previously saying, "I am going to give you a 'Timothy' who, like the Apostle Paul, you will take under your wing and train as a man of God". He looked down at me and stepped off from the platform. "What is your name?" he asked. "Tim!" I replied. Tears welled up in his eyes and his lip trembled as he placed his hand in my head and cried out to God, "Lord, baptise him with the Holy Ghost".

I had felt a real weight going out of me as I walked to the front of the church. Suddenly, I found myself strongly speaking out a heavenly language. I»m not sure if I had yet prayed the sinner's prayer. A microphone was thrust in front of my mouth. Supernatural power from God poured into me. The One who makes us complete, King, Baptiser in the Holy Ghost and fire, lover of my soul, Saviour to the uttermost, mighty Sovereign Lord and Master, had come into my heart and life. Wave after wave of the glory of God rolled over me. The search was over. The great vacuum within me was being flooded and saturated with God's fullness. I was being transformed and translated from the kingdom of darkness into the kingdom of God's dear Son. One man tried to share with me in the counselling room where we had been ushered. I only wanted to get back out there to absorb and experience more of this overwhelming presence and power.

BAPTIZED IN THE HOLY SPIRIT

Wave after wave of liquid fire engulfed me on that wonderful night so many years ago. I was 26-years-old and at the absolute crossroad of my life. Only days before, it was the effects of Tequila that satiated me as had been the case for such a long time. Now an invigorating transforming power of might and holiness seemed to be permeating every cell and fibre of my being. It was more than a 'force' or even a holy power. This invading supernatural power bought an intimacy with God that could only be coming from God himself. This saturating and thrilling experience was making Jesus dynamically real to me and bringing an understanding of Him that the natural mind could not conceive. This was indeed an immersion into the third person of the Trinity, the Holy Spirit, with an awesome sense of empowering for a great task.

What is this amazing thing that Jesus declared as the 'Promise of the Father' and John the Baptist prophesied would be a total immersion or baptism in the Holy Ghost and fire? Sadly, we as Pentecostals and Charismatic's often fail to fully communicate the purpose and impact of this enormous gift.

At Bethabara (House of Crossing) on the Jordan River, John the Baptist announced Jesus in two very different ways. As his cousin Jesus walked to him at the water's edge, John boomed out like a trumpet blast, "Behold the Lamb of God that takes away the sins of the world" (John 1:29). Every Jewish person who was there, at the place where Joshua had led the children of Israel in crossing the Jordan centuries before, must have marvelled and wondered at this statement, which encapsulated the very foundations of their faith stretching back to Egypt and Passover. For many months people had been weighing in their minds whether this prophet of God, whose booming voice thundered with such power, might truly be the Promised One. Certainly the mantle of power that cloaked him and the fearless soul-gripping words that chilled men to their bones pointed that way. After hundreds of silent years, where no prophets voice had been heard, this strange mightily-anointed warrior could almost certainly be Him for whom they so patiently waited. "Are you the One, John", they asked. "I'm just a voice crying in the wilderness saying make straight the path", he answered, "There is one coming after me who is so much mightier than me. I'm not even worthy to get down in the dust and lace His sandals. I baptize you in water for the remission of sin but He will totally immerse you in the Holy Ghost and the lightning fire of God" (see John 1:19-28). The great evangelist Reinhard Bonnke puts it this way, using John's words, "I indeed baptize you with water but He will immerse you in liquid fire". John profoundly introduces Jesus as the person of Passover and Pentecost and the One who immerses us into the fullness of God himself. He declares Him as the great Sacrificial Lamb by whose death the whole earth would be flooded with Heaven's Glory.

As I drove home that night, I was alive with an overwhelming awareness of God that seemed to have opened a new door to something so extraordinary that it defied words. "What happened tonight", I wondered, "and for what purpose?" I knew I needed to search the Word of God to fully understand. I began reading where John the Baptist called Jesus the One who would 'baptize' us in the Holy Ghost. The word baptize is the Greek word *baptidzo*, which means to whelm or to totally immerse as a cloth dipped in dye and being soaked until the whole cloth is permeated. This gift from the Father is a total saturation of our entire being in the supernatural person of the Holy Spirit and fire. Sometimes the 'and fire' is played down. The baptism in the Holy Ghost is then an immersion of every aspect of our being into God's holy and mighty self and His supernatural consuming fire. Our abilities, dreams, talents, and desires are all saturated and whelmed into God Himself. These dreams talents and abilities should ignite when flooded with the "same Spirit that raised Jesus from the dead" (Romans 8:11). We should be the innovators, inventors, creative leaders and artists. The Great Creator has immersed us in His very person. We are carriers of the resurrection life and power of Christ. I love the words of John G. Lake, the outstanding Apostle to Africa:

Sin, sickness, death under his feet. Hell itself taken captive and obedient to his word. Every enemy of mankind throttled, bound, chained by the Son of God. Mankind joined to him by the Holy Ghost in living triumph. Why if I receive the Spirit of Jesus Christ, of the Christ who is, I receive the Spirit of victory and power and might and dominion, of grace, of love of all the blessed estate of which Jesus himself is the conscious master. All these things he gives the Christian through imparting to him the Holy Ghost".

Its really much more than an 'imparting'. It is a total immersion of the Christian's entire being into the living, tangible, almighty, presence, power, and person of Jesus by the Holy Ghost.

Paul certainly expounded this in Ephesians 3:19 and 20:

That we might be filled with all the fullness of God". The Amplified Bible puts it this way: "That we might be a body wholly filled and flooded with God himself".

At the end of Ephesians 1, I read that the church is to be the "fullness of Him that fills all and in all" (Ephesians 1:23). I checked this over a number of times. Yes, we the church are to be the overflowing fullness of Christ to a dying world. We are to carry the overflowing fullness of miracle power, delivering and restoring power, power to create and shape our world and to bring the fullness of his mighty anointing into cities and nations, until His great presence floods everywhere we go. Jesus was very serious when He declared on the last day of the Feast of Tabernacles that great rivers and torrents of living water would flood out of our inner being.

"In the last day, that great [day] of the feast, Jesus stood and cried, saying, If any man thirst, let him come unto me, and drink. He that believeth on me, as the scripture hath said, out of his belly shall flow rivers of living water (But this spake He of the Spirit, which they that believe on him should receive: for the Holy Ghost was not yet [given]; because that Jesus was not yet glorified)" (John 7:37-39).

Jesus commanded his disciples to go and wait for «The Promise of the Father» (Acts 1:4). To be commanded to receive a promise seemed very interesting. Many Christians who love the Lord claim not to need this gift, yet Jesus commanded His disciples to go and wait for it. What then is this awesome Promise and what is its real purpose?

In Acts 1:8, Jesus told the disciples, "You shall receive power after that the Holy Ghost comes upon you to bear witness of Me". The word power is the Greek word *dunamis*, which is translated as power, miraculous power, miracles, inherent power, ability or miraculous enabling. Ability or divine enabling is a good translation. Here is my paraphrased version of the text: "You shall receive divine miraculous enabling after the Holy Ghost comes upon you to bear supernatural witness to my eternal existence and resurrection". In Acts 4:33 the scripture declares that with "great power the apostles bore witness to the resurrection". This divine inherent ability enables and equips us by signs and miracles to bear legal witness to a hard, cynical, unbelieving world that Jesus is not just risen from the dead but has now come to indwell and flow through our mortal bodies. The baptism in the Holy Spirit equips us to do the same works that Jesus did. It amazes me that it is the Father's great pleasure to "give us the Kingdom" (Luke 12:32).

AFRICA

In a few weeks I was headed off on the planned African adventure. I was working at labouring jobs to get finance for the trip. About three days after the dramatic night at Klemzig AOG I was working at my job as a builder's labourer when I began to shake under God's hand. It was a hot day and the work was proceeding well on a doctor's surgery we were building near my parent's home. I always enjoyed hard physical work. Finishing work at the end of a tough day's work always left me with a deep sense of satisfaction. I believe it is also a wonderful test of our character. I prided myself that I was never a 'shirker' (someone who shrinks back when we faced major jobs) and always 'pulled my weight', but this day was overwhelming. I was in the work shed shovelling cement into the barrow when I began to sob. I sobbed and wept and was too overcome to leave the shed. Thoughts of years of loose, unrestrained living flooded my mind. Thoughts of young lives led astray by my actions, young women treated as objects of lust, and drunken nights of madness, all took over my emotions. I was too distraught to come out of the shed. I would normally never let my workmates down but I simply could not face them. The tears streamed down my face. I could not stop crying. Finally, the foreman came in to see if there was a problem. I covered my red tear-filled eyes in embarrassment and told him I felt sick. I did not know how to explain the inner churning of my insides. "Go home Tim, I will take over", he said, with concern, "I will see you tomorrow". I drove to a bush place to weep and calculate to whom I should write letters and who I should see personally. The reality of a new life had come. I wanted to make restitution and to put things right. The Holy Spirit was putting His finger on issues that He wanted cleaned up in my life. I think on this day I was understanding the truth of repentance.

CHAPTER 4

AFRICA

"I have stared death in the face and he blinked first"
– Unknown

"Where is the high school teacher that was saved?" was the question asked at the Klemzig Assembly of God. The answer was that I had set out on what was planned to be a four-and-a-half-month African safari. What about Christian follow up? What would happen to my Christian walk if no one counselled me? It seemed I would probably fall away, like a fish going through the net. However, I knew I was saved. I hadn't made a decision. I'd had a dynamic life-changing encounter with God.

AFRICA

The flight from Perth, Western Australia, to Mauritius was my first international flight. I was 26-years-old. It's hard to believe that the 'jumbo' jets then looked just like they do now. Prior to this I had only flown once before. That was to Melbourne, Victoria, at 15 years of age. Our school football team flew over to Melbourne to play against Reservoir High School. I still recall the cost of the flight. It was four pounds, nineteen shillings and six pence. That is equivalent to $10 today. The Rolling Stones had just had their hit single 'Satisfaction.' They sang "I can't get no satisfaction, though I try and I try." That's over 50 years ago. It is amazing that they are still going. I wonder if someone has told them that the only place you can find true satisfaction is in Jesus.

My first international flight was such an adventure. The magnificent blue waters of Mauritius were almost iridescent as we came in to land. The magnificent bougainvillea and other tropical flowers looked and smelt wonderful. A day's exploration of this tropical paradise was invigorating. Children rode a giant tortoise near the beach, and the bright colours and excitement overwhelmed my senses. It is strange to say this, but, from the day of my conversion even the colours seemed brighter and richer. The sky seemed bluer and everything had a certain detailed look that had been lost on previous wasted years. Our next step was the city of Nairobi in Kenya, a bustling, colourful city that was so different to anything I had ever seen. Africa is like no continent on earth and Kenya was magnificent.

This was the start of another extraordinary chapter in this new life. My most valued possession there was a thick Living Bible that would be read continually across the amazing continent of Africa. Africa has a pulse and mood that is unique. The sun seems to hang blood red in the sky as dusk approaches. The people move on the streets of the cities like a river of colour. I have since travelled numerous times to this amazing continent to preach the Gospel.

In Nairobi I joined the Trans African Safari Group that I crossed Africa with. The group gathered in the hotel Chiromo. Hotels all have their own eccentricities. Our hotel was inexpensive and colourful, to say the least. There was plenty of African music, 'Tusker' beer ran freely, and prostitutes offered a 'good time' to guests. Fortunately, I was truly born again and committed to pleasing God. It was a

20-minute bus ride to the city and, as I had volunteered to protect and chaperone two of the young women on our team, we always had African men volunteering to show 'us' the sights of this great city. Certain events stand out during this ten-day period. An Indian gentleman staying at the hotel took the three of us to an Indian theatre. The movie was 'The Mechanic' starring Charles Bronson. It was in English with Indian subtitles. As the movie progressed, something was happening to me. I was itching terribly. I felt like hundreds of fleas were on the attack. I scratched and squirmed and begged God for Bronson to shoot his last victim so we could escape. I don't know to this day what manner of creatures gave me such discomfort. I think it was an attack of fleas.

The following day, after I had mentioned my great cricketing prowess, I was invited to join cricket practice for a Nairobi-Indian cricket team. I must have impressed them with my wily leg spin bowling or cavalier batting, because they invited me to come and take a school-teaching role and play cricket for the Indian side. I may have become the Sachin Tendulkar of Nairobi.

Even before I left on the four-month safari, I faced some scary situations. One night I am convinced that God spared my life. I boarded the 10-seat hotel bus to go into the city. I had planned to go to a large church that I had seen in Nairobi. The sun was setting as two young girls, almost certainly prostitutes, asked if they could go into the city. There were only three of us passengers and the driver on the bus. We had been seriously warned of two dangerous areas near our hotel. The first was a park with football grounds and the second a suburb to avoid at all cost, as the locals told us that if we ventured into that area we would be killed. As we drove towards the city, the girls were speaking to the driver in Swahili, the main Kenyan language. Suddenly, he slowed down and turned left into the same housing area that had carried such a dire warning. I questioned the uneasy driver who clumsily explained that they had to pick up some things from their house. It was now dark as we drove through streets lit by a few lights and some small fires. Then we swung into a driveway and parked behind a house. The sense of danger gripped my senses. I swallowed deeply and my eyes darted around the yard.

I knew the situation was extremely serious. I urged the driver to drive on. He insisted we wait for the girls who had now entered the house. I became very agitated. Inside the house was the sound of people partying and drinking solidly. I felt I was most certainly being set up to be robbed and likely killed. No one would have known. My first reaction was to roll a number of coins I was carrying and then wrap my fist around them. I put myself into position to drive the heels of my riding boots into those who would enter the bus. Please be aware that, as a brand-new babe in Christ and a very nervous one at that moment, my survival instincts were heightened. I asked the driver to please drive out of that place. We were both extremely agitated.

Suddenly, words flashed through my mind, "Give him money." I wondered what I was carrying in my wallet. Fumbling it open, I found a nice $US100 note, which was a decent sum in 1974. I handed it to him with a shout of, "Drive!" Off we went, to my great relief. As we drove out into the road we could hear the shouts of a group of men running after us. They shouted for us to stop, but the now financially-blessed driver drove on. I shook and thanked God for getting me out alive. This was one of a number of times in my life that God spared me. It was the first of many nerve-tingling events of the months to come. God caused, or allowed, me to face and conquer fears so that in the days ahead of me, I could handle ministry, in nations like Pakistan, India and so many others, with an inner certainty that only God can give. I think God was preparing a missionary evangelist. Since that time, I have always had a cool confidence in whatever nations God has taken me to.

Around 35 men and women, of varying ages and nationalities, met together in Nairobi to prepare for the trip that crossed the continent of Africa from East to West, then went northward to Morocco. In two former military trucks and a Land Rover all packed to the hilt, we planned to travel for the next four months from Kenya, through Tanzania, Rwanda, Zaire (Congo), Central African Republic, Cameroon, Nigeria, then north through Niger and on through the Sahara Desert to Morocco. For most of us, we were cut short three months later as Hepatitis A swept through the group in a frightening way. Fortunately, this occurred in the north of Nigeria and not halfway across the Sahara, which could have been tragic.

The group was a conglomerate cross-section of society. Among the ranks were a well-known and successful Australian pop singer, a haematologist, several seriously committed 'pot' smokers from the USA, a senior lady from England passionate about African game, a truck driver, a tough outback 'Aussie,' two mountain-climbing New Zealanders, Canadians and Dutch, all with a desire for adventure. It was not a Christian tour, with Bible studies and devotions. In fact, I may have carried the only Bible on the vehicles and, on many occasions, was one of the very few not 'stoned' on marijuana, which was claimed to be the 'best ever.' Often the supplies of 'dope' had to be smoked or eaten before crossing borders. On one occasion, a huge batch of 'hash cookies' was made. They were biscuits that used marijuana as a principle and major ingredient. One Dutch woman innocently began to eat the product, as she liked the taste, and was oblivious to the ingredients. After devouring six or more cookies, she spent the next few 'bewildered' days sitting extremely confused with a wet towel over her head.

For the next four months as a brand new Christian, I travelled through the middle of Africa with no real Christian support. I only had the certainty of my 'born again' experience, constant awareness of God's wonderful Holy Spirit, and a thick Living Bible full of words that brought courage, certainty and stability in situations that seemed slightly insane. I read and preached what little I knew. Often our truck would have more and more seating capacity because individuals escaped 'the fanatic' and travelled in the other vehicle. I was learning to preach the Gospel to a captive audience. That old Living Bible was my marvellous source of life and strength for those months.

Back in Nairobi, we packed those military vehicles with tents and supplies. We had no idea what lay ahead. I was 26-years-old, hardened from months of labouring and invigorated by this whole new physical challenge. I did not realise at the time that the experiences of the next few months were God's preparation for the wonderful soul-winning adventures that were to come in the years ahead. In Africa, I learned the importance of strong purposeful prayer, dependence on a 'quickened' word from God, and the importance of the gift of tongues, especially when facing extremely unnerving situations.

Africa is a most stimulating and stunning continent, with a beauty that consumes the senses. One image always stays with me. As we travelled from Kenya into Tanzania, we approached the magnificent Mount Kilimanjaro. There was snow on its peak as it rose majestically out of the African landscape. The sight was breathtaking. The coming week, for a Trans African traveller, was remarkable. Immediately after seeing the sun rise at this mighty mountain, we watched with fascination the migration of great herds of wildebeest. We spent time in the most marvellous Ngorongoro Crater game park, the home of perhaps the most accessible wildlife in Africa. We saw fresh kills, as whole prides of lions fed. On one occasion, we stopped the truck in the midst of a herd of 53 elephants. I remember everyone sat in deathly silence as these magnificent creatures walked past us. It only needed one of the huge bulls to become agitated and turn on us for a tragedy to occur. How incredible is the magnificence of God's creation?

From there we drove down a series of dusty roads into a fairly uninteresting area of landscape called Olduvai Gorge. This was the site where the famous archaeologists, the Leakey's, had made their 'amazing' discoveries that had supposedly proved the theory of evolution. This was the place where palaeontology had its major strike that has since totally struck out. Here half man, half ape 'missing links' (anthropoids) had been discovered. A whole family of australopithecines had been found here including *zinjanthropus boisei, homo habalis* and *homo erectus*. It was interesting indeed. Since my college days, I had always been intrigued by the theory of evolution. I had read books and seen whole articles in highly reputable publications that 'proved' Darwin's theory. Here we were at the so-called 'cradle of civilisation.' Since then, all of these findings have been totally refuted by the scientific world, as have all the 'missing links.' It would certainly save huge amounts of time and energy if scientists stopped looking and read Genesis chapter one verse one. Darwin had made it clear that, in one hundred years, palaeontology (the study of bones) would prove his theory correct. In fact, palaeontology is the theory's greatest enemy.

We set up a tent camp each night of these months of travel as we crossed the continent. Only the canvas walls of our tents protected us through game parks, bush, jungle and towns. The zipper on my tent broke in the first few days. In the jungles of Zaire (Congo), I prayed that no snakes would slither in to share my warm sleeping bag. A black mamba in the tent would not be a convenient situation. I've since been told it is a miracle of God's protection that it didn't happen.

Mount Kilimanjaro is a majestic, usually snow-capped mountain that rears up from the African plains. It is situated on the border of Kenya and Tanzania. On our arrival back there, we found a great location for our camp that gave us a stunning view of the mountain's grandeur. We set up camp in a location that would give us superb views of the sunrise on this beautiful mountain. Setting up camp late each day was a real experience. The sun going down in the west, the smell and sounds of a crackling fire and food cooking, surrounded by the vastness and rugged strength of the African bush brought a heightening of the senses. The sounds of game and the herds grazing not far from us were exhilarating. Each of us was allotted a three-hour time of guard duty during the night, as we had been warned of local tribal people who would possibly rob us. In an unprotected state, our equipment had to be watched. There was also the strange exciting sense that lions and other carnivores would be roaming around us looking for a meal.

I drew the 3.00 am to 6.00 am slot, an exciting time indeed. Two of us were awakened at 2.55 am and began our watch. A good fire burned on that chilly night and the only real action was the removal of ticks that were burrowing their little heads into our legs in search of a drink of blood. The night was still, with a bluish moonlight glow across the sky. The great black shape of Kilimanjaro dominated the land in front of us. How brilliant the sunrise would be, I thought. Warming ourselves by the fire, we talked of the day ahead. God's creation was overwhelming. Time passed slowly. More wood kept the fire crackling and we enjoyed a cup of tea. Suddenly, the roar of lions shook the entire atmosphere and shattered the silence of the early morning hours. We became aware of several hunting lions nearby. In the still night air, distance could not be calculated. We hastily threw logs of wood on the fire. I must admit, the new prayer language I had received began to be exercised. I am sure so many South African friends would mock me for going into prayer at this time but in Australia, apart from a great array of lethal snakes and spiders, camping in the bush is safe. You are unlikely to be eaten, unless you are in the Northern Territory where crocodiles abound. I think those lions were roaring, "Welcome to Africa." I have since thought of David in the hills of Bethlehem watching over his father's flocks. In those days, hungry lions, hyenas, leopards and bears roamed those hills looking for a good meal. The sound of the flocks would have drawn them for miles. Having learned to worship around the campfire, David grew in his confidence in God. With lions and bears around, he honed his weaponry skills so that he could say, "I have killed both the lion and the bear" (1 Samuel 17:36). He was prepared in those wild conditions for his encounter with Goliath.

The Africa trip for a young 26-year-old man was amazing. Twice I had the experience of a gun pointed at me. We pushed our trucks through unbelievable mud and camped in remote jungle. I recall one morning in the Congo waking up with a small pigmy man gazing into the tent. We were later invited to visit their village. It seemed very surreal at the time. In Tanzania we had climbed and slept on the rim of an active volcano and watched the bursting of lava hundreds of feet below. We hoped it wouldn't erupt that night. As we drove across the vast African plains, we saw great herds of game. We had the privilege to experience raw Africa for four months and slept in a tent every night. Every day was an adventure. It was everything I had imagined and much more. Above all that, I saw the Bible had become the highlight of the trip. The Word was opening up to me supernaturally. God's presence was constantly with me. His protective hand had certainly been with me. The leader of the tour, a big strong 'Aussie' man who I admired greatly, called me aside. He told me he observed leadership strengths in me and saw that I could handle pressure situations. He asked if I would consider taking the second role on a southern safari from Morocco and, from memory, touching Egypt, Ethiopia and south through to South Africa for seven months. My role would be to drive the second truck and be his deputy for this huge safari. I jumped at the opportunity. I planned to take some time in Morocco, then set out on this next adventure.

God knows the end from the beginning. Things dramatically changed. We were in Central African Republic when everything went horribly wrong. The leader became violently ill with strong fever and vomiting. He also became aware that his urine was like Coca Cola in colour. Hepatitis A hit the leader and, one by one, we all became ill. We had obviously eaten some infected food and, through cooking, it had spread. Dysentery, extreme fever, and vomiting took hold of most of the group. I also became extremely ill. It is very disturbing to know that you are seriously ill when you are days out from any medical help. Hepatitis A causes the liver to be badly affected. My sleeping bag was wet through every night. The whites of my eyes were yellow. By the time I had flown out of Kano, Nigeria, to London I had lost around 15 to 20 kilograms. Most of our team couldn't hold down food, as our livers were shutting down. We struggled on from Central African Republic, through Cameroons, to Kano. We had been extremely ill now for several weeks. Our next section of the trip was across the Sahara Desert. In this situation, for us to go on without medical aid could have been extremely serious or even fatal. Dehydration in the heat of the Sahara Desert was a very bad mix. I had no choice but to sell all of my camera equipment and possessions to buy an air ticket to London. It was quite a surreal feeling as we flew out of Kano International airport en route to London. The comfort of the plane seemed like a palace. Four months sitting on timber seats through the day and sleeping on the ground at night had taken its toll but now it was over. Tough as it had been, I loved every minute. It was a character-building challenge that changed me greatly. As we flew over the vast Sahara Desert, I was disappointed but very relieved. The knowledge that the Southern safari would not happen was discouraging but I knew God had a great plan.

London is truly an awe-inspiring city, but, when you are extremely sick, it can be daunting. I managed to find my way to the Victoria Street Station, and booked into a hotel. I shivered and shook for two days before taking a cab to St Pancras Hospital for Tropical Diseases. After several weeks in hospital, I was well enough to travel around England with a couple of the guys from the tour, who were also recuperating. We hired an old 'Anglia' car and drove down to Winchester Cathedral, Stonehenge, the Cotswolds and a number of famous sights. I couldn't get enough of the history of England. I had long dreamed of seeing the grandeur of London, the museums and great cathedrals. I saw things that I had only dreamed about. Standing in the Tate and National galleries, studying the works of Constable and Turner, took me back to the many hours I had sat with my Dad to look through his art books. I wished he could have stood there with me. Despite the pull to stay in London, I knew God was calling me back to Australia.

CHAPTER FIVE

PRAYER

"When we add desperation to our spiritual hunger we become irresistible to God" – **Pastor Michael Maiden**

Touching down in Adelaide was a wonderful feeling. I felt like a soldier returning from a war. I had truly experienced adventure, danger, and excitement and had loved every minute. I now weighed only 75 kilograms, which was 20 kilograms less than my football playing weight. My eyes were yellow and my liver ached. It was a number of months before I was fit enough to work and resume a teaching position. Therefore, I was required to rest to assure the liver was restored and functioning properly.

How good it was to go back to church each week to hear great preaching and to enter strongly into the real adventure of life, the adventure with Jesus. I was told to take it very quietly for six weeks, but, after two weeks of recuperation at my parent's home, boredom set in. I couldn't sit still so, against medical advice, I went back to builder's labouring. I thought that hard work in the sun would be just the thing for me. Church was marvellous. Every week goose bumps went up my spine as I sat under the preaching of the Word of God. Christian fellowship, end time teaching, long Bible discussions, and prayer meetings were so satisfying. Playing cricket on Saturday and a renewed appetite for food made life perfect. It was a real bonus to not have to sleep on the ground in a wet sleeping bag or in the ward of a hospital. I have to say that sleeping in tents has not been an attractive idea to me ever since Africa. Camping for me now is a five-star cabin in the mountains.

BACK TO TEACHING

The teaching position that was offered to me on my visit to the Education Department was something that left me stunned. "Mr Hall, we are offering you the Senior Master position in one of the state's significant country schools," said the gentleman across the desk. This had to be God. The school was only 85 kilometres from Adelaide, South Australia, so there was no need to find a new church. Of course, I accepted the position with excitement and anticipation. I knew God had blessed me with this outstanding opportunity.

The school was significant and influential and the art staff were outstanding. Our department blossomed under the hand of God. It was inspiring to watch. I knew the hand of God was on the Art Department in a way that defied description. Teachers blossomed and grew in leaps and bounds in a working environment that was alive with a genuine, extremely visible, supernatural favour. Teachers came from across the state to see our new innovations. We were a close-knit staff and God was doing significant things. I loved teaching but the passion to serve God in ministry was the thing that began to more and more to dominate my thoughts and dreams.

Church life was extremely exciting and my hunger for God became increasingly intense. I drove down to Adelaide two or three times per week, as I was unwilling to miss any meetings. I couldn't get enough of this new life. A youth camp was advertised and it had a real attraction to me. I knew something was in store and was certainly not disappointed. At this camp, the power of God was poured out in a huge way and lives were profoundly impacted. People fell to the floor; demons came out of individuals with screams as God showed His hand. I watched in awe at the demonstrations of power, as the charged presence of God swept over us in wave after wave. I knew it was a dimension of God's power, which was available to us if we were spiritually hungry. I knew that I wanted to be used of God to bring people into a real encounter with God. I saw people making decisions for God but I gained a real longing to see them encounter Him.

Upon my return to Murray Bridge, the country town where I taught, I began to pray desperately for God to reveal His mighty power to me. I needed some guidance in my quest to know, understand, and move in this 'Kingdom' power. On the following Sunday at church, I met a man whose name I understood to be Camel. He was passionate about being a carrier of the power of God. He talked much about fasting and prayer. He talked of 'fast tracking' our Christian impact by seeking God with extended times of fasting. He talked of 'Daniel' fasts, 'full' fasts, 'partial' fasts and the impact of each. In the weeks that followed he supplied me with books on the subject, then challenged me to fast two days per week. We met on Saturdays to share our faith with people. We fasted several days during the week to seek God and picked up hitchhikers on Saturdays. We talked and prayed for people on the streets of Adelaide and sought for 'words of knowledge' (see 1 Corinthians 12:8). I shared what I thought was a 'word of knowledge' with one man and boldly declared that he'd had a major crisis in his life in the month of July. He told me July had been good. I asked if it had been May, then January, and finally

December. He had experienced a few challenges then, he seemed to recall. This was about as 'accurate' as it got, but we tried hard and stepped out with little success. But we were keen to share Jesus!

PRAYER

King Solomon wrote: "If the ax is dull, and one does not sharpen the edge, then he must use more strength; but wisdom brings success" Ecclesiastes 10:10 (NKJV).

The passion to pray and touch God grew in me every day. I began to spend three days per week taking only liquids. Shortly after, I drank only water and ate for three days each week. At night, I went down to a boat ramp on the Murray River and walked backwards and forward for hours and cried out to God to feel and know His presence and power. Often this went until midnight, as three or four hours intimately and passionately locked in strong prayer with God seemed like a very short time. I was learning to live in a new place where God's presence became evident continually. I couldn't get enough of the sense of God actually in me, with me, and through me. A craving for His Word increased daily. His presence and Word seemed to be like hand and glove. I found the Word fed my soul and left this mighty deposit that I could physically feel. The Word was truly becoming bread to my soul. Just like Jeremiah it felt like "a fire being shut up in my bones" (Jeremiah 20:9).

I saw in everyday life that, even in my teaching job, the word of God helped me make decisions and handle my staff.

"Let your heart retain my words; Keep my commands, and live. Get wisdom! Get understanding! Do not forget, nor turn away from the words of my mouth" (Proverbs 4: 4-5 KJV).

The awareness of God's power was strongly with me, but it also began to stir up demonic powers. It seemed that hours of intense prayer with the understanding and the gift of tongues, coupled with a fierce hunger for God's Word, stirred things against me in the spirit realm. No longer was Christianity a nice experience at church, or a religious observance or fellowship. I intensely embraced God and His kingdom. I discovered the authority that is ours in Christ. This certainly also stirred up the enemy. Satan hates us pressing in after God. He will send his envoys to discourage us or frighten us away from our quest. He'll say you are going overboard or mad. He'll use people, often family, whose 'genuine concern' will be used to keep you from being a fanatic. I had become a fanatic in my hunger for God. It was the birth of an adventure that continues after four decades. I was totally committed to my church and its great leadership and hated to miss any meeting. I threw myself into anything asked of me but in my own time desperately sought God's face.

In my first year as a Christian I fasted many months in total and rarely prayed less than three solid hours per day. It was an absolutely thrilling adventure, far more exhilarating even than the Africa trip. How could I ever get enough of God? It was easy to identify with David's cry:

"Oh God, thou art my God, early will I seek thee, my soul thirsteth for thee, my soul thirsteth for thee, in a dry and thirsty land where no water is. To see thy power so as I have seen thee in the sanctuary" (Psalm 63:1-3 KJV).

It was during a 10-day fast where I consumed only water that I sat in my armchair in my parents' home and talked with the Lord. Without any warning, I had an open vision from God that was amazingly clear. Before my eyes was the long hallway of a house. There were some archways and on the right side some old-style hooks for coats in the wall. The walls were white and the layout of this building was totally clear. The vision was followed that night by a dream of the same place full of young people worshipping God. I knew this was my house. I had an overwhelming certainty that something amazing was about to happen. I had been boarding with a family and asking God for a place where we could minister. I knew that this place was now mine. I had the absolute 'evidence' of something 'not yet seen' (see Hebrews 11:1).

It was Tuesday evening of the following week. A prayer meeting was at the Church of Christ and a number of school teachers attended. I went along and prayed with them. At the conclusion of the prayer meeting, a female teacher turned to me and inquired, "Have you heard about the house?" I was stunned. "Only what God has shown me," I replied. She told me of a house that was available and suitable for me. It was an older brick home divided into two units. "Would you like to see it tonight? I'm sure it will be OK," she said with a smile. Although it was 9.30 pm at night we knocked on the door of 17A Sturt Street. When the door opened, I almost fell to the ground. Old coat hooks caught my eye, a long hallway with arches and all painted white. Here was the 'substance' of the vision. The presence of God overwhelmed me and I stood there with my mouth open, totally amazed. Within days, I moved into what had been supernaturally shown to me in the previous week's vision.

LEARNING TO PRAY

Here in Murray Bridge the dynamics of intense prayer had taken the central place in my life. Fasting became a true adventure. I completed my first 40-day fast while in full time work at the school. The intensity of God's presence, clarity of mind, both in the Scriptures and my work, and the overwhelming sense of His presence were totally addictive. Here in Murray Bridge, I have to confess, I became addicted to His presence and power. Every day was new and exciting, and the Word of God truly became 'food' that brought deep satisfaction. John 14:23 (KJV) says: "If anyone loves me, he will keep My word and My Father will love him and We will come to him and make Our home with him."

Often, as I prayed late into the night alone at the boat ramp, I became aware of evil that seemed to stalk me from the darkness. Sometimes it brought a strange panic sensation and my skin would crawl. I knew that God declared that He had not given us the spirit of fear, as 2 Timothy 1:7 (KJV) states that: "God hath not given us the spirit of fear, but of power and love and of a sound mind." This fear could not be from God. I wondered if this could be a small sample of the presences Jesus experienced when He went alone into the wilderness to be "tempted by the Devil" (see Matthew 4:1). Imagine 40 days alone in the wilderness where the lion, hyena and bear and legions of demons stalked in the night. Should I pull back in prayer? Was I going out into spiritual places that were unwise? The thought came strongly: "Face your fears." I remembered a road near Murray Bridge that people had declared was haunted. It seemed a murder or some violent situation had occurred on that road and strange things happened there. I decided to go down that road late at night for my prayer times in order to face my fears. Even though it was fairly nerve-wracking, I faced these fears. I walked up and down in the dark with my skin crawling and the sense of my hair standing on the back of my neck. Despite wanting to run, I pushed through my fear to praise God and declare all the Scriptures of His dominion power and dominance over all the works of the Devil. Shortly after these times, I had the privilege of casting out a demon from a person's life.

CASTING OUT A DEMON

This was a fairly comical situation in many ways. I had absolutely no idea how to cast out an evil spirit but, when a young man began to violently manifest a demon, the learning process began. He approached me one night with a look of violent hatred in his eyes and a wicked arrogant grin of sheer defiance on his face. His intent was to physically attack me. I think I reacted in a fairly natural way as I grabbed him by the arm and drove him face-down into the carpet. He wasn't big in size but I could feel a real strength in him. He snarled and growled like an animal. I pushed his arm hard up his back in an arm bar with one thought in mind: " If I let him go it's going to be wild!" I was still playing football and was in very good shape, weighing about 95 kilograms. I was at least 20 kilograms in mass heavier and struggled to hold him. At this point, I need to clearly tell you that there is no one in Scripture who took this approach to deliverance. Let me say I definitely don't do this now. Fearing to let go, I got a good leg scissors grip around his stomach. I began to shout, "In Jesus name!" Each time, he reared and bucked like a bull in a rodeo. I rode him around the room holding my wrestling grip and shouting "Jesus!" He bucked and growled and snarled until, in total exhaustion, the 'exorcism' ground to a halt. Whether he was delivered completely or not, I don't know, but I realized that this method would be abandoned.

My advice to Christians pushing out deeper and more intensely in prayer and fasting, is to be aware that you will become far more conscious of God's mighty power but you will also become more acutely aware, conscious, and discerning of demonic presences. I heard Reinhard Bonnke declare not to fear the Devil because he is just a "mouse with a megaphone."

Thank God that we can "tread on serpents and scorpions and over all the power of the enemy; and nothing shall by any means hurt you" (Luke 10:19).

The voice of God was becoming clearer day by day. I had seen the vision of the house and that had become a reality. Now I heard Him say that He would bring a group of people together who were hungry for God and that He had a plan to do something wonderful with us. I started meeting Christians who were disconnected from the body for one reason or another. I invited them to come to my home for a night of fellowship. About 12 of us sat nervously in my small lounge room. Being a new convert, of around one year with little experience, left me very unsure of what to do. I did remember those nights at the Anglican home group and prepared well for supper. I think I scrounged scones from the Home Economics department at school. From memory, they were made by year 9 students and were possibly the rejects. Enough jam and cream won the day. All was set.

We sang along to one acoustic guitar, shared several less than inspiring testimonies, then sat back and listened to David Wilkinson's 'vision' on a tape player. It sounds like something out of a museum. I had drawn the conclusion that some 'end time' teaching would certainly stimulate discussion. We sat back to listen to monumental events, which were expected soon on the planet and looked cautiously at each other. Looking back, it may not have been the ideal subject for the first night but we were enthusiastic. The tape finished. The teaching had been disturbing, challenging, and quite riveting as Pastor David Wilkerson shared his sobering visions for the future. As I began to close the meeting in prayer, I heard a strong inner voice saying, "Ask Me to come." Again I heard with certainty what I now know to be God's voice, "Ask Me to come." I told the folk that we should stand in a circle and hold hands. As we prayed, God's power filled the room like a wind. Some of the people fell to the floor, others shook and we were all totally aware that something dynamic was happening. In the midst of this activity came a knock at the front door. A shaken friend of mine stood there and asked what was happening in my house. He told me that he had been in prayer at his house and felt God tell him to come to my home. As he came in, he was overcome by God's power and fell to the floor. Within several weeks his wife and family, his mother and father, brother, sister-in-law and children, plus some friends were attending our weekly meetings and powerfully touched by God. We had mini-Pentecost at 17A Sturt Street, Murray Bridge all those years ago.

After this first night, we held regular meetings at the house that grew into what became Murray Bridge Assemblies of God Church. The meetings were always powerful, with people lying prostrate on the floor, having visions and being baptised in the Holy Spirit. The house became an absolute place of prayer. Carloads of Christians from our home church in Adelaide would arrive for our Friday night meetings and it was quite normal to have six or more people with sleeping bags stay over in my small house. Our Friday night meeting grew until people filled the lounge room and spilled out and up the hallway. It was a dynamic time, which was alive with the presence of God. Miracles and words of knowledge flowed with amazing results. One word of knowledge saw a young man confess to two bank robberies and ask us to accompany him to the police station. We took food to his cell for several days and later testified for him in the Sydney Court. Amazingly, he was released into our custody and, by a total miracle, walked free of the charges from two bank robberies. His personal surrender, total admission of guilt, and the testimonies of a number of us had a big impact, but we knew only God could accomplish this. It still amazes me to this day. Almost every person who came to visit us received the baptism of the Holy Spirit. One older man was miraculously healed of terminal cancer. Students from the school were saved and many Christians from the mainline denominations, despite being warned about us, came to our meeting anyway. God was moving and we were ecstatic.

The Friday night meeting firstly attracted top speakers from Adelaide's churches and then international speakers coming to Adelaide would be brought down to Murray Bridge to speak on Friday nights. It was evident that a church was being brought to birth.

THE FIRST CHURCH

"Despise not the day of small beginnings" (Zechariah 4:10).

As a new convert who worked as the Senior Art Master of the large Murray Bridge high school, I was stretched beyond what I thought I could handle. I quit my teaching job, which looking back was probably foolish. I now began to live by faith as I endeavoured to build a church. It was reckless and unwise in hindsight but God saw my heart. I also prayed much for someone to come who could bring clarity and stability to the Christian work which was growing and taking shape. I knew how to pray and to seek after the things of the Holy Spirit, but I was a novice who had only been saved less than two years. One day, the phone rang and a man called Brian told me that God had spoken to him about us. He said that while at Bible College in New Zealand, God had told him that he would go back to Australia and work at a church in Murray Bridge. I remember saying to him to come and be the Pastor and that I was a bit out of my depth. "No," he said, "You lead the work and we will come and help you." I asked, "When can you come?" His reply was that they could come in two weeks, on the Saturday at one o'clock in the afternoon.

"Where would they live?" was the next big question on my mind. They had two small children. I wondered if I should give them my home and I could move into a caravan. His strong words rang clear, "God will give us a house, wait and see." They had been in a 'Faith' college and they had a confidence that quite stirred me. I was extremely impressed and somewhat unnerved by a phone call I received two days before they were coming. A man phoned to ask if I was Tim Hall and if I lived in 17A Sturt Street, Murray Bridge. I replied I was and that he had the address correct. He asked, "Do you know the large house, number 18, directly across the road?" He explained that it was becoming available and asked if I wanted it? He told me that it would be available by 12 noon on Saturday. My heart pounded, the power of God gripped me, and I declared a resounding, "Yes, please!" "Would it be for Christian work?" he asked. Then, to my shock, he added, "If so, you can have it for 10 cents per year." Brian, Sue and children moved into the large property at 18 Sturt Street just after lunch two days later. The previous tenant had finished clean-up of the property only two hours before the moving truck arrived. We were stunned. How amazing were the things that kept happening so strategically?

Murray Bridge Christian Centre had been supernaturally born. I was now a Pastor of a 'huge' flock of about 35 members after I had been a Christian for less than two years. I knew just enough of the Bible to get myself into trouble but, amazingly, I now had an Associate Pastor who had actually been to Bible College. Yes, you heard correctly, he'd been to Bible College. We had hit the 'big time' now. Brian Allen had studied under Pastor Frank Houston (in New Zealand), who was a legendary man of faith and power and whose son Brian Houston is the Pastor of the great Hillsong Churches globally. Brian Allen had learned principles of faith and believing God that excited me. His understanding of these new faith principles were opening up a fresh understanding in the Word.

Now it all started happening. Meetings at the house were packed out. We had held combined meetings in the Town Hall and TAFE Centre but we were ready for the next challenge and miraculous provision. For some time, God had been stirring me about a big shed in the back yard of Brian's property. One afternoon, Brian and I started to talk when he looked me straight in the eye and told me that God had spoken to him. I knew that God had clearly spoken to me about the large shed at the rear of Brian's house. This would be our first church building. Apart from the fact that it leaned on an angle, had a dirt floor, and seemed a bit unsafe, it felt right that this was to be the home of Murray Bridge Christian Centre. We later found out that God had His plan. The property had been used as part of a ministry to Aboriginal people some years earlier.

Every great building project costs money. I have friends in ministry whose building projects have cost tens of millions of dollars. Our project was a bit less. Quite a bit less. Actually, it cost only a few hundred dollars. But with no money between us, the requirement of a few hundred dollars for cement, paint and linoleum was a mountain to be climbed. We decided to move ahead in faith. We contacted the Adelaide Church for skilled craftsmen in the area of cement work and gained volunteers from Murray Bridge. We gathered on Saturday morning with our trowels and tools for the job. By faith, and with no money, we booked a truckload of cement to put a floor in the new corrugated iron cathedral. The plan was set and the excitement grew. I was still wondering where these finances for the project would come from, but I believed that what Brian said would come to pass.

On Friday we had no finance but Brian reassured me. When he said that God would supply the money I did not doubt him much, but boldly agreed. I was fairly new at this 'faith' business. I could pray for a move of God's Holy Spirit but houses, cement and shed repairs seemed to be Brian's strength.

Saturday morning came with no sign of the money. Our motley crew of workers arrived on Saturday morning, early and eager for the task. We were dressed in our old clothes with trowels and boards and spirit levels. We used a car and ropes to pull the building approximately upright. We had everything necessary except the money to pay for the task. With the truck due at 10.30 am, the money would be necessary. Sadly, at 9.45 am our faith was being stretched somewhat. How would we pay for the cement? As Brian and I discussed the challenge, I was glad the problem existed on his property. He was the one who had learned this 'faith' stuff. He still seemed confident. I felt extremely anxious. I had pulled together this elite group of amateurs who knew approximately nothing of the task ahead and we had no money to get started. At 10.00 am all seemed lost. Often, as we step out in faith, this moment of sheer desperation is common. It seems as if it is not until the circumstances are so desperate that our faith, being tried in the furnace of affliction, produces our total trust in God! There is no other place but Him. Isaiah 48:10 (KJV) says:

"Behold, I have refined thee, but not with silver; I have chosen thee in the furnace of affliction." That was just how we were feeling!

Everything seemed lost, until suddenly, like the arrival of the cavalry, a car raced up the drive. It was driven by a man called Ron from Adelaide. Ron jumped out of his car, ashen faced and perspiring. "What are you guys doing?" he asked with an almost desperate plea. We explained the venture and the minor challenge to progress. Ron then explained that he had not slept for the last night but kept seeing us in his mind. That certainly explained his flustered state. "God told me to write out a cheque," he explained shakily. Our ears pricked up and I began to feel more excited than a long tailed cat in a room full of rocking chairs. Brian looked at me with a look of expectation and hope. Certainty began to well up in our previously nervous selves. "I have a cheque written out in my pocket for a certain sum of money," said Ron looking earnestly at us, "I have put a figure on it but not made the cheque out to anyone yet. If the amount you need and the amount on this cheque match, I will make it out to the people concerned." Brian, full of boldness, told him the figure required. With tears filling his eyes, Ron handed us the cheque with the exact amount written on it. 15 minutes later, we handed it to the cement truck driver, the cheque written out to his company. I'm not sure whether we felt relieved or exhilarated but we saw the hand of God again stretched our way.

So many incredible things happened at this time. Our foreman, as we endeavoured to lay the floor of our new place of worship, was Elio. He had been dramatically converted a few months earlier. I vividly remember hearing God speak to me, in a clear audible voice, as I prepared to drive down to Adelaide for a shepherd's class, "Don't go! I have a man I want you to meet." The impression was so strong that I drove around the town for several hours looking for the man. "Was it someone I knew?" I wondered. It didn't make sense. I went to the school, then through the main street of town, and finally gave up. I thought a pizza would be nice so I took my Bible, and sat in Mamma's Pizza Bar. As I sat enjoying my bachelor's dinner, the owner came asking if I was a Bible student. Elio told me that he had been studying with the Jehovah's Witnesses but had not found what he was looking for. We launched into an exciting and anointed conversation. I explained what we were doing, drove him to my house, prayed with him to know Jesus, and then talked about our vision for a church in Murray Bridge. Shortly after, Elio was powerfully baptised in the Holy Spirit. He became my right hand man as we worked together. Later, he became the Pastor of his own church. Elio opened a number of Christian works from Murray Bridge to the Coorong (a distance of about 150 miles) and has been significantly used of God in that area. He and his wonderful family are great friends to this day and are all serving and loving Jesus. God does not leave one stone unturned. He adds to the church daily.

What a day we had laying all the cement. We laughed, worked, rejoiced, and finished the first stage of the 'mighty edifice.' That week we were given yellow striped kitchen Linoleum for our floors, a piano, about 50 wooden chairs, and a pulpit. We even 'borrowed' a pianist from the Methodists. We were set for the grand opening of Murray Bridge Christian Centre. I suppose we should have asked the local council permission to establish the backyard church. To this day, I really hadn't thought much about it. These were unforgettable times of adventure. So much is learned in these first steps on a great journey. I can't stop smiling as I pen these words, even feeling the tears welling up in my eyes. In so many simple, yet amazing, ways God showed us His provision and love. I'm sure He smiled as He watched a band of novices who were passionate to do something for Him. He taught us well to believe and hope and against hope, just like Abraham our father in the faith (see Romans 4:16-18).

The church at Murray Bridge was established and I learned much in those years. I learned the power of prayer, and learned to step out boldly knowing God's voice. I found out much about human nature and became totally addicted to living in the awesomeness of His mighty presence. I was now also a married man with responsibilities. I had fallen in love with a young lady from Klemzig, now Paradise Community Church, and married her. She commenced a lifestyle of a wife, Pastors wife and was pregnant in one year.

OUTREACH PASTOR AT ELIZABETH A.O.G.

After two years in Murray Bridge and newly married, an invitation came to be an Outreach Pastor at a key church in Elizabeth, a suburb of Adelaide in South Australia. My senior Pastor Andrew Evans suggested it would be good for me to work in a larger situation and learn from a man of God. So we packed ourselves up in obedience to our Senior Pastor and headed for Elizabeth to be under Pastor Alan Dunford.

Pastor Alan was a strong, intimidating man of God, who had been raised on farms in New South Wales. He was strong, both physically and spiritually, with a powerful prophetic gifting. He was a man diligent in prayer and fasting who had sat under the famous Heflin family, whose prophetic gifting was known globally. We seemed to have a real understanding together in the things of God and he was keen to help build into me areas of character. His prophetic gift inspired me into a real hunger to more than see God's manifested power but also to really learn to hear the voice of God. The 'tuned ear' is so vital for effectiveness in ministry. I had a very healthy respect for Pastor Alan and was very thrilled when he asked me to host Dr Yonggi Cho (the South Korean Pastor of the largest church in the world at that time) who was coming to preach for us. Pastor Alan would be out of town ministering for another church. I was 'The Man' for the day. I hosted Dr Yonggi Cho. How amazing this was. I would get to sit with Dr Cho in the 'green room' before the meeting then walk him to the platform. What an incredible honour, this was beyond words. I had heard him preach and been so impacted by his book 'The Fourth Dimension.' I had been entrusted with something truly brilliant.

On that Sunday morning, I stood in front of the mirror and preened myself to be ready for the day. I straightened my tie and checked every detail. We wanted to look very sharp on this day. When the doorbell rang, I wondered who would be at our house at this early hour. Surely, there was not an emergency on this day of all days? It was my Pastor's son, Trevor, looking highly stressed. We were great friends, but the look on his face that day was very disturbing. «What are you doing? Service has just started!" said Trevor, "Didn't you change your clock for daylight saving?" Terror gripped me like a vice. I was an hour late. Pastor Alan's reaction would be horrendous. How could this be navigated? We stealthily moved into the church during the offering to take the seat next to Dr Cho on the platform. I took my seat and gave an air of quiet certainty that masked my inner anxiety. Trevor vowed never to tell his Dad of my major error. To my knowledge he never did. Mistakes are made by innocent circumstances sometimes. But God always works things together for good (see Romans 8:28).

I learned many things at the church and felt enriched working with a real man of the Spirit. The meetings were always charged with a sense of God's power and a great sense of expectation in the people. Sadly, circumstances outside of my control brought a sudden halt to our fruitful learning time in Elizabeth. I believe misunderstandings and jealousies of individuals caused a real move of God to be affected. Pastor Alan always told me how he wished I had never left. It is true that as one door closes another opens. That certainly became the case for me.

YOUTH REVIVAL

I took some time out of ministry after Elizabeth to prayerfully consider our next role. There was a real sense that something wonderful was just around the corner for our family. I took work as a roof tiler. It's strange looking back, but, at that stage of my life, I genuinely loved working at hard labouring jobs. These jobs included hay carting (my favourite labouring job), shed handing in shearing sheds in the South East of South Australia, builder's labouring, roof tiling and general farm work on stud cattle properties. Walking up and down the ladders and across roofs in the heat of summer was tough but enjoyable work. It is a great feeling to go home from work tired and aching. There is something noble and deeply satisfying in physical labour. I was thoroughly enjoying the work but longing to minister for Jesus. It was only a short time later that an invitation came to talk to Pastor Andrew Evans, the pastor of one of Australia's largest Pentecostal churches at that time. He asked me if I would like to take the position of Youth Pastor at the Klemzig Assemblies of God Church. For any young person who aspired to serve God, this was the golden opportunity.

My spirit leaped within me, but I wanted this to be right for our family. We now had a beautiful little girl, who we named Deborah Michele. The pull to go out and pioneer another church was strong but here was God's opportunity. We felt that it was God's plan. However, I really wanted to get away for an extended time with God to thoroughly prepare my heart and mind for something significant to happen. I accepted the position with a real expectation of a coming revival. I asked Pastor Andrew if I could first go away to pray and prepare for the task. I had always longed to do what Jesus did at the beginning of His ministry. Driven by the Spirit, He had gone into the wilderness and was there tempted by the devil (see Luke 4:1-14). I wasn't too keen on the temptation and trial of the devil, but was stirred to go out into the outback for a season of fasting alone with God.

I took a bus to the outback coal mining town of Leigh Creek, which is about 300 miles north of Adelaide, then took a light plane out to the Northern Flinders Ranges. To this day, I still go out to this magnificent mountain range to press into God in prayer. For around three weeks, I passionately and intensely sought God. His promise is that "He is a rewarder of those who diligently seek Him" (Hebrews 11:6). When alone in the mountains seeking God, I am always reminded of Jacob wrestling in prayer at Jabbok or Elijah, alone in the desolate wilderness of Tishbe in Gilead (see Genesis 32:22-32 and 1 Kings 17:1). In these desert places, these men of God transacted business with God, Elijah emerged from his intense prayer in Tishbe with an authority that would the terrorize godless king Ahab and see control of the weather system placed in his hand. When I am away with the Lord in this country, I become aware of the life of John the Baptist. He chose to live alone in the Judean wilderness separated to God in a state of intense prayer and fasting. I see John going out to the Jordan to baptise at Bethabara (the House of Crossing), with his eyes burning with a holy fire as a mighty word of holiness stunned and convicted the multitudes (see John 1:19-34). Out here, I become acutely aware of Jesus who was driven by the Spirit into the wilderness for 40 days and 40 nights to be tempted by the devil. The Scripture tells us that He went into the wilderness in the 'fullness' of the Spirit and emerged in the 'power' of the Spirit (see Luke 4:1,14). People today say that we no longer need to get alone with God in this way but, as Nike says, "Just do it." My study of revivals and the lives of the great heroes of our faith reveals people who have learned to spend great amounts of time in the throne room of Heaven 'hungering and thirsting' for a greater intimacy with the King (see Matthew 5:6).

ALONE WITH GOD

Jesus began his ministry immediately after time in the wilderness. The apostle Paul, after his baptism in the Holy Spirit at Damascus, did not "consult with flesh and blood" but went alone into Arabia for three years (see Galatians 1:16-18). It's hard to conceive, but the weighty, magnificent epistles of Paul and his monumental revelation of doctrine did not come from intense consultation with the other apostles at Jerusalem. They came alone somewhere in Arabia as Paul sought to grasp such great issues of justification by faith, the law as our 'schoolmaster', and the working of faith. It was essential for this unshakeable giant of God to be forged as a weapon, a 'sharp threshing instrument' of divine guidance and strength to the generations to come, and empowered alone with the great Blacksmith. How he must have wrestled intensely, seeking after God and drawing on his immense knowledge of the law, the sacrificial system and the teachings of Gamaliel. I picture him writing feverishly as the Holy Spirit breathed supernatural revelation upon all of his previous learning. All the mysteries and revelations of our position in Christ came flooding into his being. He must have been in a place of profound intimacy with God so that the intense treasures of wisdom and knowledge were branded into his soul like the finger of God on tables of stone at Mount Sinai. I believe the vast weight of Christian doctrine was invested into Paul during this three-year period, about which we know so little. Yet, from it we have learned so much. This should be the testimony of our times alone with God. People should know so little about the time we spend alone with Him. Yet, so much impact follows those intimate times.

The three weeks alone in the Flinders Ranges were possibly the most profound of my life. The sense of God's presence became incredibly tangible and His Word was opening with a flood of revelation. We can't buy Gods power but we can, by time spent with Him, learn to live more in that supernatural realm that is His Kingdom. As sons we can learn to operate in the full dimension of what is ours. I learned long ago that we can't buy the power of God. It is not some cheap consumer item. Simon the sorcerer tried to buy the capacity to move and carry such a powerful anointing. Peter told him God saw this as serious blasphemy (see Acts 8:18-23). The 'word' came to me as I fasted, "Don't try to buy this precious anointing. What is the difference between buying with money or food?" God doesn't want His mighty presence and demonstrated power reduced to a sideshow. We are called to bring the reality of the Kingdom of God into the midst of hurting, broken, and hungry humanity.

I returned from that time profoundly impacted and aware of a dynamic change that had occurred within me. I was ready to launch into the first 'major' phase of ministry. I sought the Lord for the best way to begin. It sounds strange to people today, but we commenced the youth program with a Saturday seminar on 'Prayer and Fasting for Revival', followed by a rally at night. Not only did the young people come out to the day of teaching, but the power of the Holy Ghost 'fell' on the place. This left young people prostrate under God's power, crying and screaming under the weight of His glory. That night was a firestorm from Heaven. Bodies fell prostrate all over the floor and demons shrieked. Our time of youth ministry was birthed in a baptism of power. The time in the mountains alone with God had stirred up a great fire in my inner man. God was now moving powerfully amongst us as a group. We truly became a group of passionate prayer warriors. We knew that we had entered into something significant.

The youth group grew very rapidly over the next year. From 17 young people in one house group, we grew to over 200 attending various home groups in the first year. Every Friday night we conducted intense prayer from 7 pm until midnight. Once every five weeks or so, we held a whole night of prayer at a farm in the Adelaide Hills. We taught the youth to move from token prayer to intense revival prayer. These nights were totally dynamic and finished with worship on a nearby hill as we watched the sunrise. There is no shortcut to revival! All the methods we can ever conceive of will not bring a mighty, surging onslaught of God›s might and power.

"If my people, which are called by my name, shall humble themselves, and pray, and seek my face, and turn from their wicked ways; then will I hear from heaven, and will forgive their sin, and will heal their land" (2 Chronicles 7:14 KJV).

Every great revival in history was birthed in great prayer. It seems that God moves on an individual or individuals to seek Him earnestly then He responds with a great moving of His revival power. We began to witness a very supernatural release of God's Spirit in the youth meetings with a flood of souls, and unique miracles of healing and deliverance. Working with Dr Andrew Evans was a tremendous honour. I was extremely passionate but needed a guiding hand. Our oversight was superb. Pastor Harry Leesement helped us to establish great follow up and discipleship for the flood of souls coming in. Our Saturday youth meetings grew until we required the main auditorium for meetings. It was a time of great impact and learning. Every phase of ministry presents its new challenges. There were many of them, but the positives, especially in the great hunger for prayer among the young people, seemed to swallow up any negatives. As we prepared for one of our youth camps, God spoke to us about a combined 21-day fast. We held a number of very fervent prayer meetings in the lead up. We knew the camp was going to be powerful when young people were 'falling out' under the power of God as they were eating the first meal. On the second night, I was leading worship when it seemed like a cloud of glory came over the whole place. I remember standing amazed as I saw flashes like mercury began to fall like rain drops across the whole crowd. As these supernatural drops came upon individuals, they crashed to the ground and lay shaking under the power of God. I watched in awe but then God spoke to me: "What you see are mercy drops but the day will come when you will stand before seas of faces and see me release thunderstorms."

STEPPING OUT

The impact of our rapidly expanding youth group created a hunger from youth groups across Australia. Invitations to preach at conferences and even crusades were coming thick and fast. It seemed what was happening was spreading as a great inspiration to many leaders. It was a time for a real expansion of thinking, dreaming and goal setting. It was at this time that the dreams of big scale global evangelism seemed like a reality. While totally dedicated to the task, I watched with interest the great evangelist in South Africa, Reinhard Bonnke ministering in a 35,000-seat tent. I listened daily to the teachings of Oral Roberts and Katherine Kuhlman on my tape player. The world seemed to be beckoning us to come. The other thing that filled my thoughts was the passion to establish churches. As I read Paul's great missionary adventures, I saw the pattern that seemed the way for us to go. He preached to masses of people and moved in mighty power, established churches, raised up leadership then moved on to the next place. The pattern seemed right for us. I noted with interest that the longest period that Paul stayed at one place was at Ephesus, for about three years. In that short time, he raised up so many disciples that the whole West Coast province of Asia Minor heard the Gospel, both Jews and Greeks. The need to raise up leaders for the next phase of the youth group became a priority. The leaders that followed the next few years were brilliant. Several of them have leadership of churches of many thousands of people today. The several years as Youth Pastor at Klemzig were a highlight of my life. It seemed that we would continue on for years, until one day in prayer, God spoke to me so clearly that I was totally overwhelmed.

CHAPTER SIX

CROSSING THE NATION

"Set thee up waymarks, make thee high heaps: set thine heart toward the highway, the way thou wentest: turn again, O virgin of Israel, turn again to these thy cities"
- Jeremiah 31:21KJV

BACK TO MY HOME TOWN

Bendigo, my home town, is a city of around 90,000 people in the heart of Victoria, Australia. It is famous for the massive gold rush of the 1850s. Tons of gold went out of the mines here. For our family, the city is incredibly significant, as I've previously shared in Chapter One. The grand opulent architecture of the main street of Bendigo dates back to the raging time in the mid-1850s, when gold fever and great wealth made the city famous.

I knew that I was going back to start a church in the Golden City. A close friend had been running a home group in the city, and he regularly asked us to come and share with 20 or so people in someone's lounge room. The evident presence of God and great demonstration of power in those small meetings pointed to something strong for the future. I thought my friend Jeff Hulls would start a church eventually. Then, in prayer, came the powerful Scripture in Jeremiah 31:21, to "return to these your cities." We decided that this was God's direction. I then chose to give my resignation to Pastor Andrew, and knock back the invitation to take on the South Australian youth leadership. It was a big decision to make, with a wife and young daughter, to leave the security and an exciting future to start a church with no backing or financial support. Sometimes in faith, you just have to jump in. A bit of wise counsel usually helps, but stubborn, slightly pig-headed people like me often just jump into a situation without stopping to do some research or calculations. With the decision made, despite some wise warnings, I gave three-month's notice at my church and started planning the strategy for Bendigo. God has His plans in these matters. We attended a South Australian Pastor's conference a few weeks before the planned move. We had no money to start the church, and our scratchy plan was not totally clear, or well thought through. During one of the meetings my old pastor Alan Dunford approached me. He was disturbed, and expressed that he had a 'word' from God for me. That day, I had felt uneasy about the timing so I walked out onto a grassy area to settle my heart. As I walked across the lawn, I gritted my teeth and thought, "We are doing this no matter what." Alan had received a 'word' at that very time. He looked me in the eye and declared, "As you walked across the grassy area, you resolved to do something regardless of the consequences." He went on to say the timing was totally wrong, and to move at this time would result in a disaster. A chill went through me. This was God. I had the Scripture burning about the cities of Victoria, yet here was a serious warning. I knew that Alan was right, yet I knew what God had spoken to me. Eating humble pie, I made the request to continue as the youth pastor in South Australia. I continued on in the role, but the urge to start a church in Bendigo burned within me.

GOD'S TIMING

I was conducting some nights of miracles in Kyabram, a beautiful little town in the lush countryside of Northern Victoria, Australia.

One night after the meeting, I sat with the pastor talking about the night and the ministry generally. The pastor began to talk about a city that was strongly on his heart. I told him that I also had a city that God had branded on my heart. "The city that I cannot shake from my mind is Bendigo," he said, with a real sense of expectation and resolve. I shared what God had said to me. He explained to me that his gifting was not breaking ground in a new place, but establishing and building once the groundwork had been laid, he could do. I knew that together this would work brilliantly. My spirit leaped as I told him of the home group and the real hunger of the folk in Bendigo. "I'll go in for a season and do the ground breaking, and then you move in and build from there," I blurted out, my heart jumping with excitement. On our return to Adelaide, we contemplated our next phase of life. We decided that we would move across to Bendigo to begin pioneering a church in this strategic city. We would work together with Pastor Ian Fenn, who would move to Bendigo once the foundation had been laid.

There were some down sides to the situation. Firstly, I had received the strong prophetic word about six months before warning us about a hasty move. We also had little money, no wage for the task, and no congregation. We only had a 'word' from God, and a strategy. Thank God for the certainty of a 'word' burning within.

THAT PROPHETIC WORD

I couldn't shake off the accuracy of the 'word' that I had received from Pastor Alan some months earlier. I respected him as a prophet whose gift was highly esteemed. I would need to see him to discuss his 'word'. I decided to phone his home and make an appointment to see him. His wife Lola answered and told me he was not at home, but would arrange for him to call me. When he arrived at his home, his wife told him that I had called. "I know what this is about," he told Lola, "It is the right time for Tim to move his family to Victoria and I feel he will be working closely with a church in Kyabram."

When I spoke with him two days later he told me what God had spoken. I was stunned and amazed at this, but his next comment thrilled my heart: "The light that was red previously is now lit up and green. Go out into the new venture with God's certainty."

Going into this venture with little money, no wage, no house, no congregation, an old car and a young family should have been a bit daunting, but we were excited and full of expectation.

GOD GOES BEFORE

On arrival, we met up with my friend Jeff Hulls who we worked with on this project. He took us to the house that some anonymous people had decided to rent for us. It was a beautiful, spacious home in a great neighbourhood. A few days later, totally unexpectedly, several men arrived from Adelaide to give us a nice car. We were also told that for our first meeting, in the small Red Cross Centre, we should expect about 30 people hungry for a Full Gospel church to join us.

COMMENCEMENT

A fifty-dollar advertisement in the *Bendigo Advertiser* let the city know that Bendigo Assembly of God Church would be commencing in the Red Cross Centre in View Street. Although it is now 30 years ago, I can still sense the fresh excitement that we felt. The big day arrived and, to our utter amazement, into the building poured 160 people. Many had come to support us from around the state. The following week we found that we now had a fully self-supported congregation of over 100 people. We were personally settled in a nice house, with a nice car and a modest wage, and a church full of switched-on and excited people.

We worked hand in hand with the Fenns from Kyabram and met regularly. We knew that as soon as the time was right, they would move down to Bendigo to build a great work. The 11 months went quickly. It was a time of much prayer, great friendships, and the sheer thrill of seeing the people of the church full of anticipation. The meetings were alive with constant manifestations of God's power. People constantly baptised in the Holy Spirit and in most meetings people were prostrate on the floor, touched by God's anointing.

When Pastor Ian Fenn and his family moved down to Bendigo, the foundations were laid upon which they would build. What a great job they did under God's mighty hand. They purchased around 20 acres of land and built a great church building to seat the hundreds of people who attended each week. Television then went out all across central Victoria and other churches were pioneered out from this strategic base. Today it is a fast-growing, powerful, and influential church in the heart of Victoria.

Not only was the church launched, but here our second child David was conceived. Bendigo has been, and still is a place of wonderful fruitfulness.

NOW WHAT? DANDENONG

The church in Bendigo was up and going. What would be next? In my first five years as a Christian, I had seen a church planted in Murray Bridge, become a married man, fathered a little girl Deborah with another baby coming, had been a pastor briefly in Elizabeth, South Australia, had seen Klemzig Assembly of God youth group grow in two years to hundreds in number, and seen a healthy church planted in Bendigo.

"Let's plant another church!" I thought. Everywhere we looked, there was a town or city with no strong Full Gospel church. With no wage, little money in the bank, and no clear direction, we should have been nervous, naturally speaking. However, the journey to this point had been so supernatural and thrilling that it was totally exciting.

In the midst of our prayers for clear direction, an invitation came to pastor a church in the outer suburbs of Melbourne. The church in Dandenong was not large, but was known to be lively with a very switched-on youth group. After twice declining, I felt God again calling me to the mountains to pray. This time I set aside 10 days to seek the mind of God.

The Flinders Ranges in South Australia is close to being my favourite place on earth. This is my favourite place to pray. It is a magnificent range of rugged mountains that rear out of the semi-arid landscape like kingly sentinels. Rocks of earthy red and ochre colour glow and change with the time of day. Distant hills and mountains are ever changing, from orange and sienna, to blue and purple.

As a teenager, I had attended National Fitness camps near Rawnsley's Bluff in the heart of the ranges. Here we camped in old military tents, hiked extensively, climbed cliffs, even slept in a cave on the peak of Mount Aleck. We had explored and soaked in the therapeutic majesty of this awesome place, but one extraordinary thing left everything of the place way behind.

We had spent a huge day abseiling on the sheer rock face of Rawnsley's Bluff. Returning to camp, we ate heartily and crawled into our sleeping bags exhausted, but in great spirits, after a big day of physical challenges.

I have always been a very sound sleeper. Nothing should have roused me from my sleep that night. In the early hours of the morning I sat bolt upright, stunned by what I saw. Standing over me was a huge white figure. Our tent was a large military tent of about ten feet high. The head of the figure was above the roofline. I remember, in my shock, either grabbing for or swinging a punch at a huge leg. The figure moved away, leaving me sitting bolt upright and stunned. I began to question what I had experienced. I was seriously shaken. Surely it had been a bad dream. Then a frightened, shaken voice from the other end of the tent asked, "Hally, Hally what was that? Did you see that? It was standing over you!"

I am convinced that I had an encounter with an angel that night, which was over 50 years ago. It's strange, but I have been drawn back to this place many times over the years. Here I have experienced a number of significant God encounters.

I was back here again for a time with God. I like to start my morning prayer times in this place watching the first golden rays of light sweeping over the huge ramparts of stone. There is a sweet, fresh smell in the air. Kangaroos graze nearby as the waking birds fill the air with a hundred songs. I drive out in the blue pre-dawn light to a different place each morning. The chilled air, the smell of pines and eucalyptus trees, and the sounds of waking nature set a marvellous atmosphere to worship and glorify our King. All of man's achievements seem to pale into insignificance as God's orchestra of light, colour, sound and smell combine. The sunrise lights His creation like a great curtain lifting over it.

The next few days were intense, as I read and prayed from sunrise until night. It was a rich time of experiencing His touch until everything turned crazy. I often drove north for a hundred or so miles to go off on dirt roads to enjoy the beauty of the landscape as I prayed. Driving off on one such road, I became aware of powerful dark presences. I felt an overwhelming sense of raw, unseen hostility rail against me. My skin crawled as I stopped the car and walked. I began to pace about, and pray fervently. As I sought God diligently, I wondered if it was something in this area, or demons sent to throw me off mentally. I really wanted to run from that place but have always believed that we must face our fears and look them straight in the eye. It was late afternoon and, rather than run, I decided to camp the night right there. All night I wished I hadn't done that. I hardly slept and spent the night feeling and sensing evil all around. I was packed and gone early to drive on to a place that was much more peaceful. For the next four or five days, I prayed much in my prayer language. No real clarity came, despite a strong awareness of the Lord's anointing. However, I kept sensing a challenge from Hell to go back to the place that had seemed so evil. I kept feeling the enemy taunt me, that if I went back there I would be killed. It all sounds weird, but it was very real to me. For the next few days, I spent intense time in prayer and the Word. The challenging taunts kept coming, "If you come back to this area, I will kill you!"

The time came to return home, but I didn't want to leave without facing my fears. I decided to go back to that area and take my stand. After some 15 days of fasting, and 12 hours per day in intense prayer I had become extremely spiritually sensitive. As I drove out to that remote area, my skin crawled with an awareness of strong spiritual hostility. My flesh was shaky but I resolved to stand against the taunts. As I reached my destination, I became aware of a mighty, surging charge of God's power pumping through me. It sounds exaggerated, but I felt that a legion of demons were all about me. I shouted that I had come in the name of Jesus, and in the protective power of His shed blood. I walked about, shouting and declaring my position in Christ. Finally, I shouted, "You've had your chance. You are a liar, Devil."

As I stepped into my car and drove away, I began to worship and shout praises to God. It became so intense that I had to stop. I ran into the bush, totally overcome with the sheer majestic anointing that was coming on me in waves. Then Jesus spoke to me almost audibly: "Drive back to Blinman [Flinders Ranges] and accept the invitation to be pastor of Dandenong Assembly of God Church. You are ready! You will face powerful forces in days ahead but you are going to see a great moving of My Spirit." The next few years would indeed be truly remarkable.

Prior to starting our time in Dandenong, I was asked to be the keynote speaker at the Victorian Assembly of God State Youth camp, which was to be held on the beautiful Mornington Peninsula about 70 kilometres from Melbourne. We commenced at the church on the following weekend.

As I prayerfully prepared for the weekend, God gave me an open vision of a map of the State of Victoria with sparks flying out in every direction from the campsite. When I arrived at the campsite, I was stunned to see a huge banner across the stage that showed a map of Victoria with sparks being scattered every direction from our campsite. The visitation of God that weekend was astonishing. On the Saturday, no one ate meals. Everybody, by their own choice and desire, fasted and sought God for something history making. God's hand came so powerfully that night that people lay prostrate on every side, weeping and crying out to God. Many had to be carried to rooms as they were unable to stand. The God encounters were powerful and launched numbers of young people into their calling. It is generally understood that this camp played a significant part in the birth of the Victorian arm of Youth Alive, an Australian youth movement that has impacted multitudes of youth for the past 35 years.

The Dandenong church wasn't large in number but it was vibrant in worship, openness, and hunger to experience God, with a great youth group who knew how to pray earnestly. They were under the direction of their youth leader Malcolm Fletcher, who is now a significant global minister who works extensively across Europe. They had been eagerly asking for a pastor with a passion for the moving of the Holy Spirit, an ability to work with youth, and an evangelistic zeal. I guess I ticked the boxes. This church loved to pray. Every Friday night was a half night of prayer from 7:00 pm until midnight. Scores of people showed up to pray every week, excited and full of faith. On Sunday afternoons, 60 or 70 young people went up onto a nearby hill to passionately pray for the

Sunday night meeting. Later, rapid growth forced us to move into the large town hall nearby, and out of the old Presbyterian Church building we were in, which was now packed and overflowing. On Sunday nights, a rostered team of around 20 young people would go down into lower rooms during the service to cry out for the glory of God and for great miracle power to flood the meeting. I remember having to send messages downstairs to ask them to cut the decibels down a little, as their passionate prayers were so loud that it became distracting as we preached. I still see these meetings as among the most consistently mighty church meetings I have ever witnessed. Our street evangelism team saw genuine miracles every Friday night, as they ministered with strong prayer backing. People came from all over Melbourne to taste the power of God that invaded every meeting. The church grew rapidly, and our family grew by one with the arrival of David Stewart William Hall. Some 35 years later, he is the pastor of a great church in Adelaide and travels across the earth preaching the Gospel.

In a short two years I learned so much about what can be achieved by a powerful praying church. When we arrived, around 100 people attended the first meeting. Well over 500 attended the last one. I watched a powerful youth group hit the Dandenong streets like Holy Ghost commandos. The miracles they saw were amazing, and each week they brought in rows of young people into church.

Today the multi campus church is several thousand strong and impacts the world with a very strategic missions program. It is great to still work alongside the church 35 years later. Two years ago, we worked together on major crusades in Myanmar (formerly Burma). Faith church, as it is now known, invested large finance to set up the meetings that took place. Planetshakers injected finance and sent the band, which was a massive draw card, and I had the privilege of preaching at the crusade meetings. Tens of thousands turned to Christ and mighty miracles occurred. We did the same thing a year later, with even greater results. What a joy it is when churches and ministries work together. Thank you, Pastor Matt Heins.

Two years in Dandenong were a thrilling, extremely productive, and fruitful time. The church grew very rapidly, and from it we saw a number of churches commence in other locations. I travelled across Australia and New Zealand preaching. I was very involved in the formation of Students for Christ in the universities and I was also active, alongside my youth pastor Malcolm Fletcher and Pastor Gary Watts, in seeing Youth Alive Victoria established. And now we had two young children. Little wonder, I wound up totally exhausted with extremely high blood pressure. I think, looking back, I faced some burnout. As young preacher, your enthusiasm often surpasses your wisdom and can lead to hasty decision making.

DECISIONS, DECISIONS!

I decided to hand on this thriving, passionate church that was so filled with greatly talented and hungry people who loved us. I accepted the position as evangelist to the state of Victoria. I felt that I had given everything to the task and was too exhausted to keep pushing. This decision was one that I regretted for a number of years. Even on our last night, as we looked at a healthy night crowd of over 500 people (a good-sized church in the early 1980s), I squirmed inside at the decision we had made. There is a knowing in God that something of great destiny rests on certain churches. I wondered deeply inside if I had walked away from the chance to build a great church that would shake nations. God knows it all and, under the leadership of Pastor

Alun Davies and Pastor Matt Heins, the church is a powerful work that touches the nations with a significant mission emphasis.

Restlessness and regret create double-mindedness, which stunts and stifles our capacity to move forward with confident effectiveness. A year later, despite having great meetings across the state and nation, the passion to build something haunted me.

GEELONG

We decided to start another work in the city of Geelong, Victoria. I felt like I was, to some degree, grasping at straws at this time. No longer was single-minded clarity my strength. Things seemed a bit cloudy and unsure. I longed to feel the pulse, excitement, and inner satisfaction that we had at Dandenong. There is no better place to be than with a highly charged group of intensely praying, fully committed Christians who are powerfully impacting their community. There seems to be a point of critical mass that comes, in a strong growing church, where the church seems to develop its own powerful momentum in God. I knew we had touched that place in Dandenong and I had stepped away. I wanted it again, but also realized the passion and diligence required to be back at that place. What did God want? Had I missed a huge God-given opportunity? Did God want me to be a pastor or touch the masses in evangelism? I was in a very hard place of regret, double-mindedness and deep self-searching. The one great thing, which seemed to keep things stable and moving, was diligence in prayer and fasting. No matter what our thoughts and emotions might be doing within us, God remains totally stable and totally committed to guiding our path clearly.

Every morning I would drive up to the You Yangs Ranges national park about 25 kilometres from Geelong. Here I found a huge flat rock from which there was a great view of the region. This was a great place from which I intensely cried out to God in prayer. For hours each day, a powerful foundation was laid for the church, the region, family and the future. Some really wonderful people in Geelong, who also loved to pray, surrounded us. Soon there were groups of us praying on this big rock. The meetings in the Geelong West town hall were exciting and we soon had a strong foundational group of over 100 people. Our stay in Geelong was only a year before accepting the invitation to take on a key church in Perth, Western Australia. The Geelong church is today the thriving Gateway Church, led by my friend Pastor Phil Ward who has built into his people a wonderful missions passion. During our short time in Geelong, I know we laid a great foundation in prayer for the church and did our best. It was personally a very unsettled, and difficult time of deep self-searching and striving to clearly understand the real purpose we were called to. Double-mindedness was my biggest challenge for a number of years. I believe I made hasty decisions that, in hindsight, may not have been wise. God tells us in the book of James that double-mindedness causes a person to be "unstable in all their ways" (James 1:8). Paul certainly lays out his attitude on the subject: "I therefore so run, not as uncertainly; so fight I, not as one that beateth the air" (1 Corinthians 9:26 KJV).

PERTH

"Wake up and marvel at the raw beauty of the Nullarbor. Taking its name from the Latin meaning 'no trees', the ancient Nullarbor conjures the sense of limitless space and time."

This advertisement for the Great Southern Railway expresses the strange beauty of the landscape that that we viewed from the comfort of our first class carriage as our train sped through mile after mile of treeless red land. How vast is this great brown land of "drought and flooding rains." For two days we looked out of our window at treeless land covered only with blue grey spinifex bushes. Occasionally, kangaroos bounded away majestically as we thundered past. My mind went back to the day I sat in a timbered carriage with studded leather seats as a ten-year-old boy, rattling away from all I knew, to an adventure in a whole new place. Our family were doing the same all these years later.

Hyde Park Assembly of God was strong, conservative, and historically the most influentially significant Pentecostal church in Perth. The people were a wonderful group, loving, immensely proud of the church's history, and very set in their ways. Overall, our time in Perth was wonderful. Every emotion was experienced from hilarity to utter frustration. The church was very much board run and I know my approach to ministry was received with great joy, and some nervous uncertainty. The board were really special men, who I loved and appreciated. They were thrilled with the moving of the Spirit of God, but not open to the ideas that I felt God had given me. The church loved to pray. The youth blossomed and we mentored some key young people who God had placed strongly on my heart. Each one of them is now doing significant work for God on an international scale. Despite enjoying being the pastor and loving church life, my enemy of double-mindedness kept me from fully engaging my heart and seizing this opportunity with the single-minded passion of heart needed to build a major, impacting work for God. I know the passion and resolve that has gone into building the great churches we see in the world. I am in total admiration of the people God has raised up to seize the challenge. As I travelled, I knew the gift that operated through me out in the field was strong and immensely satisfying. My dreams were of great crusades, in huge open fields, with multitudes streaming to the altar. In my heart, the desire to pastor a very large church was very stimulating. However, in the intimacy of prayer, my constant cry to God was for a powerful, impacting anointing that would shake and impact nations. Reinhard Bonkke was my hero and everything he was doing, I watched with huge interest. I was caught in a place that demanded clear and certain decision making. We had enjoyed the few years in Perth but knew that in order for the church to go to the next level, it demanded very strong steps that required a steely resolve, which would result in definite collateral damage.

CROSSROADS

The Stirling Ranges lie about 350 kilometres south of Perth. These rugged peaks rear up out of the landscape with a regal splendour. Bird life abounds as a vast array of species wheel and shriek overhead, filling the air with an orchestra of life. These mountain ranges also have unique smells of the various shrubs and foliage. Kangaroos bring a unique smell that blends with that of the foliage. You may have gathered by now the great love I have for the Australian bush. Alone with God in the Australian outback is the nearest place to Heaven.

I needed to finally do away with this uncomfortable uncertainty restricting our impact for God. I remembered how Abraham was "fully persuaded" regarding God's purpose for him (see Romans 4:21). I believe that, when we are single-minded and clear regarding our destiny, we are unstoppable. My mind flashed to the Tower of Babel and the oneness of mind and purpose that caused God to say:

"Behold, the people is one, and they have all one language; and this they begin to do: and now nothing will be restrained from them, which they have imagined to do" (Genesis 11:6).

Napoleon wrote, in 1831 in *Maxims of War*: "Hesitation and half measure lose everything in war."

I am convinced that any great achiever in any field of human endeavour has locked onto their purpose for life like a laser. I once heard Dr Yonggi Cho talk of seizing your vision like a stranglehold and being ready to die with it.

DECISIONS

"Come now, and let us reason together, saith the LORD" (Isaiah 1:18 KJV).

The time had really come to clearly establish God's future plan. Being a pastor was enjoyable without really beginning to satisfy the deep craving within that constantly filled my thinking. My constant prayer was for a nation-shaking anointing. The continual dream was to follow the example set by the great Reinhard Bonnke. Again, a great pastoral opportunity lay before me. Alone in the mountains, I pressed hard after God with passion of soul. It is said of Epaphras that he fervently strove in prayer for the Colossian church. The Greek word translated "to fervently strive" is *agōnizomai*, which means "to *struggle*, literally (to *compete* for a prize), figuratively (to *contend* with an adversary), or generally (to *endeavor* to accomplish something): - fight, labor fervently, strive."

"Epaphras, who is one of you, a servant of Christ, saluteth you, always labouring fervently for you in prayers, that ye may stand perfect and complete in all the will of God" (Colossians 4:12).

I did not want to miss God's plan in Perth, as I had some real images of the steps that would take the church to a major place of impact. I was also very aware that the required steps would not be popular and the church would need to be shaken to the foundations. It was very clear that people would be hurt and serious collateral damage would ensue. God's voice came very clearly: "If you are to take the next step it will require total commitment and strength. People will be hurt as they struggle to grasp your decisions. You will have to make a long-term commitment if this is your choice. Your passion for evangelism has been birthed by Me and I will bless you greatly if you follow this course."

Could I commit to being a long-term pastor? Was this the great passion of my heart? I could not make the commitment, so I decided to single-mindedly pursue global evangelism. I had some regrets and questions as we drove out of Perth after several great years and the birth of our third child Ashleigh Jessica Hall.

CHAPTER SEVEN

MOUNTAINS AND VALLEYS

"Now therefore give me this mountain, whereof the Lord spake in that day" – Joshua 14: 12-15 KJV (words of Caleb)

Immediately after our arrival back in Adelaide, life changed dramatically. We sold our beautiful new home in Perth, left a solid wage, and with a young family, launched passionately into this new endeavour. Doors opened across our nation and into Asia and the Pacific islands. It was hectic, exciting, and a huge challenge financially. I was very ambitious and desperate to make an impact. I prayed much and travelled extensively. Although we began to be supported by one of Australia's top fine artists, few churches were aware of the amount of money that was required to run the ministry. At times, even our costs were barely covered as I ministered for numbers of days. The financial pressure began to build on my family.

At this point I would like to speak to young ministers who are stepping out. Make sure to guard your family. Be very wise in how long you leave your wife to handle the pressures of the home base. Financial stress is a great enemy of the family.

Looking back, I feel I could have done many things differently if I knew what I know today. It is truly said, "You can't put an old head on young shoulders." The children were 11, 7 and 2-years-old when circumstances, related to ministry and my driven approach, reached a place where my wife could no longer cope. I found myself alone with the three children. I do not blame her in any way, but look back and see many challenges that are strong examples to anyone in ministry. Never let personal ambition or quest for success in ministry take your eyes away from your family's needs, especially those of your wife. Ministry can leave your family with a sense of abandonment if we selfishly follow our own course. The same can apply for a businessman or any husband. As men, we can be so brutally insensitive. When I finally saw the signs, it was too late. In fact, it was an encounter with God that revealed my situation.

DREAMS SHATTERED / TRAGEDY

I was ministering in a large hall in Papua New Guinea. The hall was packed with hungry and excited folk. Hundreds stood outside in the rain. It was on this wet and rainy night in the highlands of that extraordinary land, that we witnessed the most remarkable release of Gods miracle power that I had ever seen. I was elated. A few days later, I was to be on the Island of West New Britain to preach at my first great outdoor crusade meeting with five or ten thousand people attending. I lay on my bed filled with expectation. Here, I felt that mass evangelism would begin for us in a huge way. We had broken through into the big dream. I knew that from here we could launch big outdoor meetings through the South Pacific islands. Support was coming, and businessmen would back our strategy.

I went to bed that night with a great sense of satisfaction, but with no idea of what was about to unfold. I woke in the middle of the night, sweating profusely and with my heart pounding. A strange sense of paranoia gripped me. I am not a fearful person, but I shook and perspired with a sense of hopelessness. I sensed, "Your family is under siege. Tim, go home." The words kept coming, "Go home!" I paced the room, knowing the truth of the situation. I hadn't really seen this coming, but I was awakened with a huge shock. I had no choice but to follow this impression and fly back to Adelaide. I phoned the missionary friend in New Britain and explained that I had to let them down and fly home. His words to me ring in my ears, even today: "Tim, I would have been very disappointed unless God had already told me that it concerned your family. I have been teaching the people regarding the vital importance of putting your family in their right place." I flew home that day.

Back in Adelaide, and now aware of my situation, I strongly endeavoured to make the changes needed. However, it all came to a head. I was heartbroken and alone with three small children to support. Immediately, I did the only thing I knew to do, which was to go into extended fasting and much prayer. These were the darkest days of my life, in fact, all of our lives. I know that for my wife it was also a terrible heart-wrenching time. The world seemed upside down for all of us.

FAITH TRIED

Many months before, I had been invited to conduct a large crusade on the island of Guadalcanal in the beautiful Solomon Islands. I felt emotionally ill-equipped for the task, as I struggled with a constant depressive sense of grief and even despair. To be perfectly honest, I would far prefer lining up on the front row of a raging battle than going through the pain of a torn family.

No matter how hard I tried, I was unable to find a replacement for these meetings. I braced myself and flew out to preach in this famous World War ll theatre of battle. As we flew in over the blue tropical waters, on approach to the very airstrip that had been the central piece in the brutal fighting here in 1942, all I could think of was the pain we were all feeling. Preaching was the last thing I wanted to do but here we were.

I sat in my hotel room trying to mentally and emotionally prepare for this five-day stadium crusade. I listened to some classical music and tried praying about what to preach. God would have to be my strength. Everything seemed empty. "I can't really do this," I thought. I cried out to God to be my strength. At around 4:00 pm the presence of God suddenly filled my room. It felt like the unseen hand of God had unscrewed the top of my head, and a feeling like warm honey poured through me from head to toe. It was the most extraordinary sense of love and strength combined. That sense has never left me from that day.

As we drove to the stadium that evening, the pain seemed so far away. In my weakness I could feel His strength being perfected.

"And He said unto me, My grace is sufficient for thee: for My strength is made perfect in weakness. Most gladly therefore will I rather glory in my infirmities, that the power of Christ may rest upon me." (2 Corinthians 12:9).

The smell of the hibiscus flowers filled the air. The sight of the people walking to the stadium and great lights illuminating the field and sky sent a thrill through me. We began that night with a small group of about 2,000 people in the large stadium, but it totally changed. The crowds grew each night as God's miracle power flooded in night by night. Thousands were swept into the kingdom. Crutches were discarded, and the deaf heard as Heaven was released in Honiara.

My fondest memory was of a comatose man carried in on a stretcher, and laid at the end of the platform. People fanned him and pushed the crowd back from him. As I prayed for a group of deaf people at the other end of the platform, I heard a roar of excitement. I looked about and saw the man carrying his rolled-up bed. In the next few minutes, sticks and crutches were discarded and some were thrown onto the stage. This was one of the great nights that are emblazoned in my memory.

On the last night, the ground and grandstands were full. There wasn't even space for an altar call. That night, around four thousand people responded to the call for salvation. They were standing all around the fence line. I remember, as I walked among them, the sight of their tears, which streamed over their dark faces like mercury under the reflection of the lights. Until then, I had never seen so many commitments to Christ in one night. I knew that night, this was the reason I was walking on planet Earth. Any doubts as to my call vanished. I have clearly understood since Guadalcanal that international power evangelism is my God-given destiny. I believe I became addicted that day, to seeing multitudes of souls filling altars of churches and stadiums on every continent.

I returned to Adelaide with very mixed feelings. I had experienced the most amazing few days of God's visitation at the darkest time of my life. I had sat with the Prime Minister of the nation and was told that these meetings had been the greatest event since their independence in 1973. I returned to my challenges at home. As the plane flew homeward over the blue Pacific Ocean, God again spoke to me. I felt the challenge to pull out of ministry and do all I could to see the family restored. In my quest for ministry success, lack of sensitivity, moodiness and frustration had been a huge factor in our situation. I felt in many ways I deserved to be in this place. I decided to cease ministry for an indefinite season.

WHERE NOW?

My pastor was shocked when I told him that I was pulling out of ministry indefinitely. The question arose as to how to earn a living.

GOD ALWAYS PROVIDES

I went into a time of extended fasting and praying much in the language of the Spirit. I asked for clarity for our financial situation as I had taken time away from ministry. On a stunning day, I stood on a hill and talked to the Lord, looking over the beauty of the Australian landscape before me. The ochre, sienna and faded blue grey colours were stimulating. The sky was a rich blue and some white cockatoos screeched as they flew overhead. I was lost in God's creation. Without any expectation, I suddenly heard God say, "Pick up your paint brushes." It was almost audible. I knew I had heard His voice.

I drove immediately to my parents' home and asked my father, who was an extremely accomplished water colourist, if I could borrow some of his paints. I purchased some watercolour paper and brushes and spent the next three days painting landscapes. One of them was about 20 inches by 15 inches and another six paintings were about 14 inches by seven inches. As I painted, I felt elated and had a real sense of God's touch on each piece. Colours flowed like nothing I had done before and I was excited.

I went down to the picture framer with the paintings in hand. The framer, who is now a great friend, looked hard at them. "Who painted these?" he asked, as he adjusted his glasses and looked closely at each piece. When I explained that I had done them, he politely asked if they were for sale. He was interested in the larger one and asked its price. "One hundred and fifty dollars," I replied." At that moment, two ladies from church walked into the shop. After greeting me, they set their eyes on the paintings and asked, "Can we buy them?" I sold them three paintings at $50 each. These were small and quick to paint. Right on cue, an art dealer walked into the shop. He stood at the counter and glanced across the paintings spread out across the glass. "Who is the artist, and are they for sale?" he asked. His next questions were, "How much? Can I buy them? Can I commission 20 of these small ones per week at $50 each?" Over the next twelve months, I painted and sold over 1000 paintings, mostly these small 'pot boilers', as we called them. My friend Steve Lubcke began to sell art for me. And that year we sold several large pieces at around $700 each as well as the 20 small ones per week.

For the next year, I didn't preach a sermon. I painted late into the night to produce enough pieces for the dealer to choose 20 for the week. I also worked numbers of days as a tree lopper with a great group of friends who had set up a company called Mr Clip. The children were in a Christian college and I set my work time around them so that we would have plenty of quality time together. I even outsourced all my washing and ironing, and paid for it with paintings. Later, when the door opened to preach and the ministry began to grow again, art became a vital part of all we do. Today, exhibitions continue to be held to raise money for ministry projects.

Since 1989, we have sold over 3,500 original paintings, produced over 20 limited edition prints, and have work hanging in the homes of leading sportsmen, internationally famous musicians, Prime Ministers and politicians. My work hangs in game parks in South Africa, corporate offices, and homes across the world. I've had the privilege of illustrating a number of books and made as much as $55,000 for one painting. It all started from one clear word from God: "Pick up your brushes!" God spoke to Moses and asked what he had in his hand. When He breathes on anything, even a boy's lunch, it multiplies exponentially.

SMALL STEPS BACK

"If you can't fly, then run, if you can't run, then walk, if you can't walk, then crawl, but whatever you do, you have to keep moving forward."- Martin Luther King Jr.[6]

"Never give in – never, never, never, never, in nothing great or small, large or petty, never give in except to convictions of honour and good sense. Never yield to force; never yield to the apparently overwhelming might of the enemy." - Winston Churchill [7]

"Never give up on something that you can't go a day without thinking about." - Winston Churchill [8]

After all the thrill and success of the Solomon Islands campaign, it was over a year until I preached again. We attended church each week, and the art kept us financially comfortable, but the family situation was complicated and painful for all concerned. The dream for the nations burned as strongly as ever but the focus was on the family. In 12 months I didn't preach anywhere, not even at a home group. It was a time to knuckle down and show some character.

Despite the uncertainty and emotional pain, we had as much fun as we could and I remained very passionate in prayer. Each day I spent at least three to four hours in focused prayer. There was never there a doubt or question that our destiny was finished.

One pleasant Sunday morning, as I sat in Paradise Assembly of God Church, the Lord spoke to me, "It's time to preach again!" I felt very stirred within. Then, as we walked out of the church, Pastor Andrew Evans turned to me and declared, "It's time to preach again, Tim."

A few weeks later, I had the opportunity to preach to a small congregation in the outback mining town of Coober Pedy. Wikipedia describes this hot outback town as follows:

"Coober Pedy is a town in northern South Australia, 846 km (526 miles) north of Adelaide on the Stuart Highway. According to the 2011 census, its population was 1,695 (953 males, 742 females, including 275 indigenous Australians). The town is sometimes referred to as the 'opal capital of the world' because of the quantity of precious opals that are mined there. Coober Pedy is renowned for its below-ground residences, called 'dugouts', which are built in this fashion due to the scorching daytime heat. The name 'Coober Pedy' comes from the local Aboriginal **term** *kupa-piti*, which means 'boys' waterhole'. Opal was found in Coober Pedy on 1 February 1915; since then the town has been supplying most of the world's gem-quality opal. Coober Pedy today relies as much on tourism as the opal mining industry to provide the community with employment and sustainability. Coober Pedy has over seventy opal fields and is the largest opal mining area in the world."[9]

The people there mainly live in underground houses, which are cut into the hillsides. Sandstone is very strong and stable, and these homes are wonderfully and consistently cool. Temperatures there are so brutal in summer that most people leave during that time to avoid the temperatures of 50 degrees Celcius (that's 122 degrees Fahrenheit) and higher.

It was a big change from the last huge crusade in the lush green island of Guadalcanal in the Solomon Islands. This was no mass crusade, but a chance to preach to about 60 hard working mining people in the harshest outback conditions that you could find anywhere on the planet. I preached and shared with real enthusiasm and then watched God fill that underground building with the same power He had demonstrated in the Solomon Islands. The meeting wasn't big in number, but it was big in God's presence. The people were blessed and so were we. The 846-kilometre drive each way was well worth it. One great lesson to learn is to give our all to whatever opportunities come our way.

From this point, preaching opportunities started to come, mainly from smaller churches. Gradually, larger churches, who heard of miracles and moves of God's power, began to open their pulpits. It was humbling, but at times we have to grit our teeth, hold on to God and our vision, and refuse to give up. This is when the Lord infuses some steel into our soul. Never give up. Never, never give up. Sir Winston Churchill's quotes always inspire and amuse me.

"Success is the ability to go from failure to failure without losing your enthusiasm" - **Winston Churchill** [10]

VARIETY IS THE SPICE OF LIFE

Over the next two years, we were pastors for a short time in South Melbourne, Victoria, taught high school classes in Bendigo, Victoria, painted and sold art, produced limited edition prints, and did some reasonably large crusades in Papua New Guinea, Fiji, and then South America. I tried to do everything to keep my children excited about serving God. When we lived in South Melbourne, we visited Luna Park, a historic theme park, every Friday night. We ate plenty of not so healthy food, and they travelled with me every chance they could. It was fun at Luna Park to ride the same roller coaster that my father had, while he attended Wesley College in the early 1920's. We cut a recording in a small karaoke booth at Luna Park. We usually sang out the old song 'Under the Boardwalk', which was recorded by the Drifters and the Rolling Stones in 1964. They are probably not great lyrics for a Christian family.

After speaking at large outdoor campaigns in Karachi and Lahore in Pakistan, God clearly spoke to me to return to Adelaide. These meetings were brilliant, as God healed people on every side. So many crippled people were healed and these meetings were certainly one of the great highlights of my life. With the excitement of Pakistan fresh in my mind, we packed our few possessions, left Melbourne, and headed back to Adelaide.

BIG SEASON

"And let us not be weary in well doing: for in due season we shall reap, if we faint not" (Galatians 6:9).

Pakistan had been amazing. It was extremely challenging and somewhat intimidating to minister in a Muslim nation. We ministered in a massive tent-like structure that was said to hold 20,000 people. By the end of six nights the crowd was huge, with the tent packed and big crowds outside.

The miracles were numerous and undeniable. Little children, who were previously crippled, walked across the stage fully restored. I vividly remember a young woman weep as she testified of the great miracle she had just received. Her arm had been twisted and deformed since birth, but she stretched it forth completely straightened and restored. This was the first of three very successful campaigns we have conducted in Pakistan.

We came back to Adelaide where we settled for the next 20 years.

"Pray, preach and paint" became something of a catch cry. Business people began to support our ventures, especially one of Australia's top artists, Kevin Charles 'Pro' Hart. For many years, 'Pro' and his wife Raylee were our major ministry supporters. 'Pro' had been a miner in the famous city of Broken Hill in the far western outback of New South Wales. The 'Silver City' has produced massive tonnage of silver, lead and zinc since the first discoveries in 1853. 'Pro' has been called the father of the outback painting movement. His art captures the colours and mood of the Australian outback in a profound and often humorous way. His early life was spent on a sheep station near Menindee in outback New South Wales. He worked for years in the Broken Hill mines where he sketched and cartooned in every break. He was constantly designing and creating all manner of inventions. The miners called him 'The Professor', which later became the name that everyone used: 'Pro' Hart. Sadly, my great friend and supporter passed away on the 28th March, 2006.

I met 'Pro', a committed Christian, somewhere in the 1980s. I had admired his work greatly as an art student at the South Australian School of Art in the late 1970s. He captured the mood of the Australian outback in a most fresh and invigorating way. He loved the ministry and had his own strategy of evangelism. He painted flowers or dragonflies on the covers of small Bibles. He painted them dozens at a time. The paintings were quick, brightly coloured, abstract works. Inside, he put an insert that said: "This is an original 'Pro' Hart painting. It will fade away but the Word of God will never fade away." He painted thousands of these that have been distributed all over Australia and way beyond.

'Pro' was genuinely excited about our overseas campaigns and became our biggest financial supporter. On the phone, he regularly asked, "Where are you going next, mate? I have paintings for you." I would then drive to Broken Hill to spend great quality time with 'Pro' and we often painted together. Then, on my return, I sold the paintings to a variety of buyers. The times I spent with this amazing man remain an absolute highlight of my life. He was an absolute genius with a hilarious sense of humour. Through the many paintings he gave to our ministry, over a period of 15 or so years, we were able to see over 600,000 souls saved.

In 1993, after four years as a single man with young children, I married Jacquelyn Ann Hancock. Jacque had been alone for over ten years, and had intended staying that way, until God told her that she would be marrying me. I was living in Melbourne at that time and she wondered if she was hearing correctly. She put out a 'fleece' to the Lord as follows: "If this is you Lord, they will be back from Melbourne within 24 hours." That next day she was at work in a well-known Adelaide jewellers' shop when, to her utter amazement, my daughter Deborah walked in and said that we had moved back from Victoria. She was stunned but still put out a few more most interesting 'fleeces' in the months ahead (see Judges 6:36-40). It is hard to believe that this was nearly a quarter of a century ago. Jacque occasionally reminds me that our honeymoon was a campaign in Estonia accompanied by my son David. This is not entirely true, as we had a few days in Glenelg after our marriage. But then we did head straight off to Estonia.

The meetings in Estonia were held in the former Communist Cultural Centre in Tallinn. The walls of communism had just come down. A huge sculpture of Lenin's head stood arrogantly at the front of the building. I remember vividly the grey skies, snow and hundreds of heavily-clothed people who poured into this large, dark, timber-lined cold, and impressive building. It had that stoic communist feel. So many communist leaders had propagated their godless, humanistic philosophies in this building that we brought the message of the living, risen Jesus in. The exhilaration of preaching in that place was huge. I could sense the heart of God towards these dear people, who had suffered long under the steel fist of Soviet domination. How miraculously God moved during that week. Doctors came and sat in the meetings and tried to understand how these things were happening. Each night the crowds packed in and God's glory filled the place.

One highlight of the time in Estonia was the chance to preach on a Russian nuclear submarine base to officers, wives and children. About 200 people sat in the building and waited to hear the gospel. I wondered how many were hearing about Jesus for the very first time. Amazingly, after I preached, everyone in the room accepted Jesus as Saviour.

The opportunity came to preach in a Russian prison just out of Tallinn. It was a freezing day and I well remember wearing thermal underwear. This was the first and last time! The prison was something straight from a movie, a grey, foreboding, concrete 'hellhole'. The man in control of each cell block was the hardest, toughest prisoner. I learned that 43 people had been murdered there during the previous year. We were guided through doors and corridors to the prisoners' chapel. The place was cold and very intimidating. We were ushered to the Christian chapel unsure of what to expect. We were stunned as we entered. It was brightly coloured with beautiful paintings covering the walls. It was brightly lit and a handmade heating device warmed the room. It was God's oasis. The presence of God filled the air as prisoners filed in. They did not have particularly warm clothes and the temperature outside was well below zero.

I preached on the subject "The Bible, the prisoner's book." I talked of the epistles written in cell blocks and the many heroes of faith who had been imprisoned. It is always a joy to see people turn to Christ but that day, in that grey horrible place, it was a special thrill. I will never forget one prisoner, with eyes filled with tears, handing me a card on which was written, "I was in prison and you visited me." As we walked out to freedom it was a joy to be out of that ugly place, but my heart went out to those committed incarcerated Christian men who brought life to those tormented inmates.

In 1993 we were greatly impacted by one of the most anointed and inspiring men I have had the privilege of knowing. Dr Rodney Howard Browne is a unique gift to the Body of Christ whose passion is to not just see multitudes saved, but to bring a God encounter to multitudes across the earth. His ministry greatly inspired us as a family and, through our time with him, many doors have opened for us across the USA.

Through the late 1990's to 2002, we worked out of Adelaide and based ourselves in our old home church (then called Paradise Assemblies of God). It was great to be around family and be able to be support to our aging parents. My son David joined the ministry team, and began to successfully handle key areas of the work. We travelled widely and, in the late 1990's, we ventured into television with our programme 'Only Believe' shown across Australia, New Zealand and the South Pacific. It was later broadcast out of Hawaii to millions across the subcontinent. This was an exciting venture and very fruitful, particularly through the South Pacific. On the one Papua New Guinea channel, 'Em TV', our 7:00 am Sunday morning spot helped open the nation to us. It amazed us how powerfully our programme prepared the ground for crusades. As a result, over the past 36 years, I have preached 42 times in this amazing country. Through the 1990's and 2000's, we conducted revivals across Papua New Guinea, from the coastal cities, to the highlands, and out to the provinces of Bougainville and New Britain. We ministered a number of times in the National Stadium in Port Moresby, and were even invited by the PNG government to come with our expenses fully paid for by them. On this occasion, ministering with Pastor Joseph Walters, we had powerful meetings in the National Stadium for 23 nights. During this time, we saw a huge harvest of souls and great miracles. Doors opened to preach in the Solomon Islands, as well as Vanuatu, Fiji, and Samoa. God has given us a supernatural love for the South Pacific that has never waned. Even today, as I sit down to write this in my hotel in Port Moresby, I have just preached last night with the Planetshakers team to over 60,000 people in the totally renovated National Stadium on Papua New Guinea's great day of National Repentance.

In 2002, we decided to plant a church in the south of Adelaide. I took six months off the road, rented a building for offices and the Magic Millions horse auction building to plant a church. I guess, if Jesus was born in a stable, we can plant a church at a racehorse auction room. The church grew slowly and steadily to over 300 people who were passionate to pray. Six months of being a pastor and not travelling, again left me in no doubt about our call. We gradually handed the work over to David, who has now joined the church to another and is building a dynamic church that touches the city of Adelaide. Grand children came into the world and ministry continued to expand.

In 2012, we received a great offer to move to Melbourne to be based in Planetshakers Church, which is led by Pastor Russell Evans and his wife Samantha, who is Jacquelyn's daughter. We felt it was a sound move at our age and thought it would give David a chance to really stretch out in ministry in his own right. During the past four years, huge doors have opened as new frontiers present themselves. On a few occasions, we have worked together with the Planetshakers band, to see nations touched significantly. Perhaps one of the great blessings and a key to personal growth has come from our involvement both in lecturing in the Planetshakers Bible College, and taking large teams with us on major campaigns. I will share some thoughts on this in the next chapter.

IMPACTING NATIONS

The last 40 years are for me a blur of great revival meetings in stadiums, football grounds, churches, conferences and prisons. Every year, the world seems to get smaller and smaller and the excitement of preaching the gospel in nation after nation never loses its thrill. It's been amazing looking back at the places where we have ministered over the years, from the Australian outback in summer heat to a Russian nuclear submarine base in the Baltics. From the tropical tip of Australia's Arnhem Land in the Northern Territory, to the beautiful Apple Isle of Tasmania, through outback desert regions, classically Aussie towns and our own world class cities, and across every continent (except the Antarctic), we have preached thousands of sermons. Ministering to Australian Aboriginal people in the heat of summer with temperatures of 118 degrees Fahrenheit tests the stamina, especially swallowing a fat blowfly or two as I preached. The South Pacific nations mentioned above have been a highlight and big focus for us. At this point it seems right to share some of the highlights of our crusade ministry over the past 40 years.

CHAPTER EIGHT

CRUSADES

"If you want to catch fish, don't throw your net into a bath-tub." – Reinhard Bonnke

PAPUA NEW GUINEA

People often ask me, "Which country has been your favourite place to preach?" Others ask, "Where have you seen the greatest fruit for your work?" Naturally every place is unique and special, but one country has held a very special place to me personally, and our ministry team. It is the beautiful, tropical country located north of our great brown land of Australia, Papua New Guinea.

It's called 'the land of the unexpected.' It's a tropical nation of around 7.2 million people made up of a major land mass and a number of islands. Amazingly, of approximately 3,000 languages on planet Earth for the seven billion inhabitants, over 860 of these languages are found in Papua New Guinea. In World War ll it was a significant theatre of war. The names Kokoda, Buna, Sanananda, Milne Bay, Sattelberg and Gona became part of Australian folklore, as fierce, unrelenting fighting from 1942 to 1945 saw Australia avoid invasion by Imperial Japanese forces. To this day, thousands of war relics litter the country as a reminder of a war that saw over 127,000 Japanese soldiers die in this nation during those brutal days. Thousands of Australian, American and Papua New Guinean soldiers also died in this harsh, unforgiving, jungle theatre of war.

WORLD WAR II

As a young boy, I vividly recall the reunions on Anzac Day of my father's unit from the war. The first one I recall was in 1958 in Adelaide. My Dad took me to the Anzac Day march through the city. Thousands of men marched that day, many in uniform. Row upon row of men, who had fought during World War I in Gallipoli, France and Palestine, marched proudly. Here were men, now in their sixties, who had endured the horrors of the Ypres Salient, and of France, as artillery and machine gun fire decimated whole Battalions of men in hours. Here were men who had climbed the slopes of Gallipoli, as bullets whizzed about them like swarms of hornets. Here were men who had faced death from flying metal, dysentery, or a knife, club or bayonet in hand to hand combat. I viewed every one as a hero. Then came the thousands of men from World War II. It had only finished 13 years previously so most of these veterans were in their early forties. I waited expectantly for my father's unit, the 2/16th Field Company. They were a unit that had served in North Africa, in the Libyan and Egyptian theatre, and in Papua New Guinea. Dad had talked to me of the great fields of land mines they had laid around Mersa Matruh and the seven-month period during which they were constantly bombed. There was something about seeing Dad march past that day that caused me to stand up on the inside with certain strength. My Dad was my hero, quiet, polite and strong. To this day, I do not have one bad memory of this great man. One hour before he died suddenly, aged 87, I went to his home, embraced him and told him that no man could have been given a better father. Tears ran down his face. These were the last words I ever spoke to him.

At the reunion party, I heard the men talk of their times together, especially in Papua New Guinea. My father often talked of the appalling conditions they experienced as they spent many months building a road from Wau, near Lae in Morobe Province PNG, to Bulldog in the Gulf Province. At heights of 3000 metres, they cut and blasted their way, in tropical heat that was rarely below 85 degrees Fahrenheit and with temperatures at nights dropping so low that frosts were common. He talked of being in wet clothes constantly. Like most of the unit, he contracted malaria as well as chronic dermatitis and brucellosis (a disease associated with cattle). He spent months recuperating at the Heidelberg facility in Melbourne. His love for Papua New Guinea was great and he delighted to talk of the 'Fuzzy Wuzzy Angels', which was an endearing term for the national men who acted as stretcher-bearers to bring wounded Australian troops down, through the most treacherous and arduous terrain, to medical aid. He was a fine watercolourist who painted many scenes of the terrain and people. He also brought back a beautiful black wood bow and arrow set given to him in the gulf province. As a boy, I often tried unsuccessfully to shoot rabbits with this weapon. I still have it in my possession. I developed a love for this nation as a boy, little realizing the scores of times that I would travel to this 'land of the unexpected' ministering the love and power of Jesus.

SMALL BEGINNINGS:
MY FIRST INTERNATIONAL MEETINGS

I had settled into my position as youth pastor of the Klemzig Assembly of God church (now called Influencers Church in Adelaide, South

Australia). God was moving powerfully as the youth group grew very quickly. Our church was one of Australia's largest, led by Dr Andrew Evans who had served as a missionary in PNG with great impact. His father T. L. Evans had been one of the great pioneers in that country, who introduced the baptism in the Holy Spirit to the people. I received an invitation to do a large National PNG youth camp in the area where Pastor Andrew had been a missionary. My first overseas opportunity brought an urgent sense of sheer exhilaration to my heart. This was the beginning of my call to the nations.

My first memory of PNG was the heat and humidity. The air seemed to burn my throat as I breathed but my heart beat with excitement. The air was filled with the smell of the hibiscus flowers. All around, great coconut trees reached skyward. Everywhere there was the excitement of a new, very different culture. It reminded me of Africa and, to a lesser extent, India from my trip several years earlier. It looked like Mauritius, yet this place had a rawness and a sense of belonging to me. It was as though it had been preordained long before, that I would be here. I loved the country from that first day and that passion increases every time since.

The youth camp was the biggest thrilling opportunity of my life up to that point. Young people came in from all over the nation. The air was filled with an electric sense of expectation and God's presence. When they began to worship in the first meeting, the hair on the back of my neck seemed to stand up. Their hunger and passion for God was overwhelming. On and on they worshipped, many with tears streaming down their faces. I recall ministering on the baptism of the Holy Spirit and watching what seemed like an avalanche of power leave hundreds weeping and sobbing all over the floor. This was my introduction to international ministry and it was exhilarating. I became further addicted to seeing people encounter

God. I was learning that the greatest thing I could do in ministry, was to bring a strong word from God and the anointing for great personal encounters. The camp stays emblazoned in my mind after all these years. The sight of these beautiful brown skinned people weeping and crying out to God has continued all these years. My last role on that trip was to preach on Sunday at the Wewak Assemblies of God Church. About 400 people were in attendance and 20 were saved and a deaf ear opened. I was so excited. I look back on it and think about recent nights when many thousands have come to Christ, with hundreds miraculously healed. The excitement remains the same today. In campaigns over the years it has been a common sight to see hundreds of people swept to the ground under the power of God as He swept like an unseen tsunami over the great crowds.

Here in PNG I met my lifelong friends Joseph and Margaret Walters. Together, Joseph and I have conducted over 40 campaigns across the nation. Joseph's impact has been huge, so much so that several years ago he was honoured with an MBE (Member of the British Empire) for his Christian services to his nation.

It is strange how a nation can so impact your heart that you feel compelled to return again and again.

WAR ZONE – BOUGAINVILLE AND PAPUA NEW GUINEA

A brutal civil war had raged in the Papua New Guinean province of Bougainville for 10 years. Huge copper deposits had been discovered in 1969 which had led to massive mining projects that provided much of PNG's GDP. Hostilities arose to such a place that, in 1988, a conflict arose that ran for 10 bloody years. Over 2000 Bougainville Revolutionary Army soldiers and between 15,000 and 20,000

Bougainvilleans had died. In 1998 came a temporary ceasefire and with it, a personal invitation to preach open air meetings across the island. During World War II, this state had been the scene of massive fighting between Australian, U.S. and Japanese forces. Again it was seeing bloodshed and great pain. Virtually all of the government infrastructure had been destroyed. Hospitals, schools, and anything that seemed to be governmental was destroyed in what seemed to be ludicrous acts of violence. Even running water and electricity were gone in some areas where we preached. The massive copper mines that had brought so much wealth to the nation were now shut down. The rebel army hid out in the bush, continually fighting guerrilla conflicts. With the ceasefire, came a small chance to flood the island with God's love, and a miraculous demonstration of His power. We must grab opportunities when they come. I wondered what we should expect. No outdoor meetings of this kind had occurred for decades. What would be the response? Teaming with Steve Blake (Liberty for the Nations) we arrived in Buka, Bougainville. Steve's crew had bought over a Land rover vehicle, dentist's surgery, and items such as clothes. We had no idea what was ahead, yet within us we had a huge sense of expectation.

We were far from disappointed despite a few minor obstacles. Because of the civil war, Papua New Guinean soldiers were set up in all strategic areas. There were sandbagged areas and military establishments around us. We were approached as we surveyed the football ground where our first meeting would take place here in Buin. The place is famous for being only a short distance from the wreck of Admiral Yamamoto's plane, which was shot down during World War II by American Corsair and P 39 fighters sent from Guadalcanal (Solomon Islands) to intercept him. Japanese Admiral Yamamoto was the architect of the infamous Pearl Harbour tragedy. An officer approached our team as we looked over the platform, sound system, and lighting that was being fine-tuned for our opening night. "You cannot preach here tonight," he declared strongly. "What is the reason for that?" we asked. He then explained that their security vehicle had been stolen at gunpoint from the platform a day or so previously. It is strange when the Holy Spirit grabs hold of your vocal chords. Without thinking, and with a real sense of God's authority, I looked him square in the eye and said, "We will be preaching here tonight. Losing your vehicle is your fault, not ours. Anyway, most of your men are backslidden Christians and you all need God. So be here tonight!" He hung his head and said, "Yes, Pastor." The soldiers indeed filed in that night and took their seats. From night one God's power flooded the football ground. It was supernaturally glorious. God was invading a place where war, distrust, and fear had stalked them. It was primitive and uncertain, but thrilling. I vividly remember the sound team fanning the smoking amplifier with banana leaves. An opportunity then came, to minister in villages of the Bougainville Revolutionary Army. This area had been totally closed for years. The only way to travel to the first village was with a large hired tip truck. About 40 nationals were on the back of the truck. I love these wonderfully crazy and surreal things that accompany evangelism to the nations. In the first village, the vehicles bore witness to previous actions. Bullet holes were evident in most of the cars and trucks. The young, stoic-faced, heavily armed men viewed us with suspicion at first, then began to open to us. The places where we stayed at first had bullet holes through the walls and no electricity or running water. However, night after night, great numbers were saved and miracles flowed. Personal comforts seem unimportant when God is doing powerful things all around us. The last four or five nights are etched in my mind indelibly. We crossed the sea at Buka to another island. I remember the terrain clearly. It was covered in huge craters where Australian Naval ships had shelled the Japanese mercilessly in 1942 or 1943. The barrages must have been horrific. The whole place was covered in these craters. 6-inch and 8-inch naval guns from Australian cruisers had incessantly pounded the Japanese troops. Now we sensed God's heavy artillery being put into position for the night ahead. I love the South Pacific islands, but especially late in the day. The smell of hibiscus flowers and the sound of insects begin to stimulate the senses. If the meeting is in a stadium, the lights and walking crowds thrill my soul with holy expectation.

This was a day meeting with a small but expectant crowd of several thousand people. As I stood up to preach God spoke to me, "Preach in Pidgin today." I can communicate conversationally in this PNG language but had never preached a sermon using it. It was amazing and somewhat supernatural how strongly it flowed. Most of the crowd responded to the call for salvation. God again spoke, "Wave your hand over the crowd." With that, God swept over the crowd, sweeping them to the ground weeping and crying out to Him, as miracles, deliverances, and healings broke out en masse. A few days later the same thing happened with a crowd of around 10,000 people in the open air in Buka. Most people were swept to the ground as God breathed His supernatural breath over them. This same manifestation continued happening with bigger and bigger crowds across the South Pacific.

PORT MORESBY, PAPUA NEW GUINEA - GOVERNMENT SPONSORED

We were ministering in the National Stadium in Port Moresby some years ago. We have conducted 40 campaigns in Papua New Guinea over the years, taking the National Stadium seven times. On one occasion the PNG government, concerned about crime in the city, actually invited us to come for a campaign in the Stadium. They paid for the air tickets, stadium and hotel. Amazingly, the Deputy Prime Minister was our driver. Working together with my friend, national Pastor Joseph Walters, the greatly anointed meetings extended and ran for 23 nights with an estimated 30,000 commitments to Christ. I have worked together with my great friend and associate, evangelist Joseph Walters for many years now. Joseph's wife, Margaret always greets me as 'Tambu', we are family with them.

On this campaign great crowds poured into the stadium and, sadly, we had brought only a small healing team with us. An anointed healing team is essential when conducting major meetings. Looking at a sea of faces was great but how to effectively reach them all was the burning question. We normally pray mass prayers for healing, but a strong healing team moving into the crowd seems to greatly increase the number of miracles. I had heard previously that a large contingent of national people had walked for a week across the rugged Owen Stanley Ranges on the famous Kokoda trail. Brutal fighting had occurred on this track between Australian and Japanese soldiers in World War II. If Port Moresby had fallen, Australia faced imminent invasion. The courage and sheer determination of our soldiers (many with little training) against a powerful and highly combat hardened Japanese army has made Kokoda part of our Australian folklore. To walk it is tough and demanding, but to walk it while fasting makes it amazing. These marvellous people had walked this mountainous, demanding track while fasting for the meetings. I invited the Popondetta people who had done this trek to come up onto the platform. They crowded onto our platform. I wanted to pray for them and introduce them to the people. Before we had a chance to pray, the glory of God fell on them and they began to crash down all over the platform. They shook and trembled as the torrents of God engulfed them. "Here is your healing team," I heard the Lord whisper. Each night as we came to the time of healing I called the 'Popondettas' to the platform. They stood facing tens of thousands of expectant people. As I prayed a mass prayer, the prayer team immediately launched into the masses. The miracles of God were everywhere. This is the Mighty Holy Spirit glorifying Jesus and bearing witness to the fact that Jesus has been raised from the dead. These beautiful people were filled and overflowing with the miracle grace and power of Christ.

AFRICA

I fell in love with the continent of Africa when I was part of the trans Africa safari back in the 1970's. The opportunity to preach in Africa took that excitement to a new place. In the past 18 years it has been a joy to preach in Zambia, Botswana, Namibia and across South Africa. It has been my joy to minister with some of the giants of the faith in Africa, especially South Africa. It was Pastor Ray McCauley who first opened the nation to us. The great Rhema Church in Randburg was my introduction. This great church and ministry has been instrumental in multitudes of the nation turning to Christ. The opportunity with Pastor Ray opened the door to the powerful CRC movement, founded and led by Pastor At Boshoff, who is one of the greatest men of God I have met. For the past 16 years I have ministered in his incredibly fast growing movement. The mother church today is numbered well over 40,000 in attendance with huge churches springing up across the nation. "Win the lost at any cost" is their catch cry. I love ministering in these churches for many reasons. The excitement and passion generated in their meetings is totally inspiring, the strength of leadership pushes me to a new level, and the knowledge that the huge harvest coming to Christ in every meeting will be meticulously followed up. I really want fruit that remains.

ZAMBIA

African people are by nature enthusiastic. The children, no matter how poor their background, seem to squeeze every ounce of excitement out of life. Singing is a way of life and big outdoor meetings are an event that brings out their passion.

We were in Lusaka for a big outdoor crusade meeting some years ago. Evangelist Benny Hinn had been in the city a few months previously. I was feeling somewhat intimidated following one of the great healing ministries of our time. When we arrived at our accommodation, it was the country palace of President Chiluba. Monkeys swung in the trees outside the windows and armed guards roamed the compound. It was quite an experience ministering in the parliamentary building and having the president's wife sing in one of the meetings. After a big march, with thousands of noisy and very excited Christians, we began a series of large outdoor meetings. I vividly remember seeing strange things happening in the crowd as I preached. It looked like whirlpools in different areas. It was people who were manifesting demon spirits. As they lashed out, kicking and clawing, the people scattered from around them leaving these strange effects across the crowd. Each time this happened, they were carried out to a tent where an experienced team were setting them free in Jesus' name. The lesser kingdom was giving way to God's mighty kingdom. It was dusty and dry naturally, but a living river flowed supernaturally. People screamed and jumped with delight as the healing power of God swept over them. Every miracle is another clear declaration that Jesus is alive from the dead. The joy of watching people streaming to the altar turning to Christ never ceases to thrill my soul. Here, in a totally unique and new environment and culture, we watched in awe as thousands of folk came to Jesus in the same way that we see it across the earth. Africa is unpredictable in many ways, but is one of the greatest harvest fields of souls on the earth today.

PAKISTAN

When an invitation came to conduct large outdoor meetings in Pakistan, my mind was flooded with a wide range of thoughts. I couldn't think of anyone I knew in ministry who was preaching there at that time. I wondered how large outdoor meetings would be permitted in an Islamic nation, and the question of safety and security needed consideration, especially if a team was involved. If we are to touch the world in a major way, we will have to be willing to put ourselves in areas of risk at certain times, but wise calculating and planning cannot be overemphasised.

Karachi metro is a massive, sprawling dusty city with an estimated population of over 23.5 million people as of 2013. That's a density of more than 6,000 people per square kilometre (15,500 per square mile). It is called 'the city of lights' and 'the city that never sleeps.' Arriving in these great cities bombards the senses with noise, colour, smells and awe as multitudes throng about on every side. The traffic is an endless, seemingly-confused mass of horn-blasting vehicles emitting clouds of blue grey fumes that seems to move with their own strange sense of purpose. The driver starts pointing out the large hand-painted billboards advertising the meetings. The excitement begins to build.

We ministered in a massive tent-like structure that was said to hold 20,000 people. By the end of six nights, the crowd was huge with the tent packed with big crowds outside.

The miracles were numerous and undeniable. Little children, who had been previously crippled, walked across the stage. I vividly remember a young woman weeping as she testified of the great miracle she had just received. Her arm had been twisted and deformed since birth, but she stretched it forth, completely straightened and restored. The manifestation of God's presence and power had been amazing.

This was the first of three very successful campaigns in Pakistan.

INDIA

India has been an exciting challenge, with many large outdoor meetings before numbers ranging from 5000 to 100,000 people per night in attendance. Hindu people seem to be especially excited by God's miracle power. The truth is that we all are!

GUJARAT INDIA

"Mumbai (formerly called Bombay) is a densely populated city on India's west coast. A financial centre, it is India's largest city. On the Mumbai Harbour waterfront stands the iconic Gateway of India stone arch, built by the British Raj in 1924. The city is also famous as the heart of the Bollywood film industry. " [11]

Time spent in the huge pulsating, colourful, overpopulated Indian cities produces an onslaught on the senses that can be totally overwhelming. Personally, I thoroughly enjoy the excitement and energy, the continual noise, exotic aromas and the sea of humanity that moves like a tidal swell. I vividly recall spending three days in Chennai watching Australia and India play out an absorbing Test cricket match. Sitting in the well-used grandstand among a host of cricket fanatics in stifling heat and humidity with incessant beating of drums is something you dream about, especially if you have eaten a big super supreme pizza before bed. The fans' friendly but passionate taunting, with hastily drawn pictures and signs held up in front of us depicting Australia's certain demise, brings a crowd interaction that is especially designed to suit my personality. One must temper responses playfully but strongly. It makes for a hot, sweaty, tiring, humorous day

Driving in India is an art form that I have no desire to explore personally. Night driving is an adventure that challenges your nerves and can make you very aware of your mortality.

Driving out of Mumbai, through the maze of dusty streets with the vast tangles of overhead power lines, totally ignored car horns blaring, and brightly dressed industrious people swarming like ants, seemed to intensify the excitement we felt about the major meetings awaiting us in Gujarat. Everywhere something grabbed your attention. It could be five people on a motor bike or a bus so filled with people that they hung over the sides. People pulled incredibly loaded carts while a new Mercedes darted around us. Day turned to night as we headed out on the four-hour drive that turned into eight hours. India's economic revival means that the roads are filled with fast moving trucks with tired irritated drivers pushing to finish this job and start the next. In among the modern trucks and cars are older, battered, unlit vehicles, thousands of motor bikes, rarely with just the rider, carts loaded with sugar cane stretching across the road, buses packed unbelievably, and carts pulled by animals.

First time travellers hold onto the dashboard with white knuckles, and gasp in unbelief at the amazing creative driving techniques revealed all around and the incredible timing that is shown to pass vehicles and narrowly avoid death. These events occur about every five minutes or so. It is quite amusing.

This drive was quite riveting to say the least. I thought Heaven was close about 15 times that night, but we arrived at our beautiful accommodation in rural Gujarat at some horrendous hour. The house amazed us. It was a magnificent home, made with much black marble and exquisite fittings and art work. It sat close to the centre of a village that seemed unchanged in hundreds of years. It was set in a scene that was breath taking. From the balcony the next morning, we watched ladies getting water from a very old pump and carrying home the filled, heavy containers on their heads. Children washed water buffaloes in the crystal clear waters of a sparkling river that wound away to distant mountains over what looked like a fertile flood plain. I sat drinking chai and looking over the scene, aware of a sense of God's power that seemed to come over me in waves. We had been told that this huge gathering was happening in this rural area because the cities would attract major persecution that was strong at that time. We were told to expect crowds of 100,000 people per night in this seemingly remote rural area.

Over the years we have ministered in many revival campaigns in India. Always our God of miracles comes in great power, demonstrating to multitudes of hungry people that Jesus Christ is indeed raised from the dead and alive across the earth today. I could write of so many of these campaigns, each unique in the miracles and great numbers of people turning from darkness to light. Hinduism offers little to its vast numbers of followers. What a joy it is to watch, as God opens deaf ears and crippled people stand up on newly strengthened and restored limbs.

The drive out for the first night was full of expectation for our team, especially as we watched in amazement the procession of vehicles and walking families streaming towards the great gathering. The crowd was huge. It seemed to stretch so far back. What a privilege to preach to so many people. What a joy to be carrying the power and Word of God.

The estimated size of the crowd was 100,000 people. This was a sea of colour that seemed to be pulsing with a great expectation. How powerful is expectation! It is such a joy to come into a situation where the organisers have planned thoroughly and prayed with great purpose. Expectation is not just for these great events but local churches must foster and build that sense that something is going to happen every time they are together. Many churches are so predictable that no one in the congregation has any anticipation. They know clearly what every meeting will bring. This is not the nature of God. I want to wake every day saying, "God, please shock me today!" As an evangelist, I want that expectation to grow stronger every night of a series of meetings, building on the previous night.

This great meeting in Gujarat remains in my mind for its great size but more so for the urgent sense of expectation that I felt. The church in this State had experienced huge persecution. Many of the pastors who were present had been threatened or beaten. There was a great sense of purity and powerful commitment, which mixed with God's mighty power, saw a huge harvest of souls, miracles and profound encounters. All through the crowd people shook, trembled and fell as waves of glory swept over them.

THE GREAT CHALLENGE

Every time we have visited India we have been thrilled at the great hunger for God and openness to the miraculous. We have also been aware of the teeming masses of humanity who have never experienced the mighty life-changing touch of Jesus. We have to look, not at what we have seen, but at what lies ahead that needs to be achieved. I remember vividly when Reinhard Bonnke moved from the big 35,000-seat tent to the open field crusades. God spoke to him and said: "I am taking away your sickle and giving you a combine harvester!"

It is time, as Jesus said, not to see the harvest four months away but to "look up now and see that the harvest is white unto salvation" (John 4:35). Joel well described these times when he spoke of "multitudes, multitudes in the valley of decision!" (Joel 3:14).

We live in the greatest day of opportunity ever seen in the history of the church. It is the day allotted for the most passionate, anointed, fearless preachers to step out, with great planning and prayerful purpose, into the greatest harvest field ever imagined. There will be great cost and a great need for courage but the Psalmist David well prophesied: *"My people will be willing in the day of thy power"* (Psalm 110:3).

MYANMAR (BURMA)

Going into previously closed nations is always a thrill. The sense of uncertainty and possible danger heightens the senses and stirs the prayer life to a new level. Myanmar had been under an oppressive military junta from 1962 to 2011. After this, significant reforms have been slowly introduced, particularly since the opposition party returned to power in 2015. Although the military still exercise a level of control, the nation has slowly come out of some decades of isolation. In 2014, we began working with Faith Church and Planetshakers Church (both from Melbourne) to conduct mass crusades in this beautiful land. The Planetshakers band ministered in worship and I preached in Rangoon and several other key regions.

As we flew into Rangoon, we saw below us exquisite golden Buddhist temples. The urge to minister the reality of Christ began to pulse on the insides. Our team, numbering about 30, were filled with expectation. The following day we flew to a place called Kalaymyo, where we would conduct a mass outdoor crusade for three days. Before that, we went out to a region that had been closed for years. We knew that a Bible College had been established and that they had organized an outdoor campaign meeting.

No one warned us about the 'deadly' road that we took to our destiny. Our team took the trip in a large tourist coach. No one mentioned until our return that buses, cars and motor bikes regularly went down the sheer cliffs at the side of the road. Looking out of the bus window revealed the sheer drops straight down with no rails. Evidence of collapses of the road in different sections didn't enhance great confidence in me. I tried to imagine how it would be in winter rains.

That night we were stunned as around eight to ten thousand people jammed into the prepared area. The band ministered and the young people roared with thrills and excitement. As I preached, I felt the freedom of a new day in this nation. Thousands gave their lives to Jesus that night.

The following day, as we drove back on the treacherous road, we stopped at a fairly primitive cafe for lunch. I don't know what we ate, it may have been dog. Whatever it was, that night many of the team were seriously ill. I have rarely been ill on all the campaigns we have done, but this night I was in a very bad way. I was due to preach in Kalaymyo the next night but was vomiting all day. I couldn't even stand but was determined to preach. An hour before the meeting, I remember crawling out of the bed, showering and dressing for the meeting. I wondered how I could preach but was desperate to do so. As I walked up to the steps to preach, suddenly I felt violently ill and projectile-vomited under the steps then preached flat out for 40 minutes. The miracles over the next few days were amazing. Most of the huge crowds committed their lives to Christ.

We travelled to Rangoon for several afternoon meetings in a large auditorium that seated about 6000 people. We would minister during the afternoon from 2.00 pm till around 4:30 pm. These were brilliant times with so many saved and healed.

At the start of these meetings, some people conducting a large outdoor crusade a few hours away approached me. Unfortunately, their preacher had visa problems and they asked if I could replace him. They said it would be a two-hour drive straight after we finished the Yangon meetings and that around 25,000 people would be waiting. After preaching and ministering in Yangon, several of us drove out on the two-hour drive to a place we had never heard of. After the two-hour drive became four, we arrived. I stepped up onto the platform, preached, prayed then travelled four more hours home.

Thousands were saved and healed so, when asked if we could do the same the next day, we accepted immediately. The following day was again amazing. In two days we had ministered at four crusade meetings, driven at least 14 hours and seen at least 15,000 people saved and hundreds of miracles.

Myanmar had been a rugged and incredibly taxing, challenging and exciting time. Naturally, when the opportunity came to do the same thing one year later, we jumped at the opportunity and saw another amazing two weeks of ministry.

VANUATU

The sea was unusually warm and the clouds seemed somewhat foreboding as we sat with Pastor Steve discussing plans for a citywide campaign in Port Vila, Vanuatu. Little did we know that within a few days a massive cyclone would rip these beautiful islands to pieces. Money was raised, houses restored, and the desire of our hosts for a real crusade of hope remained on the table. We were able to raise the money for a sound system, pay for lights and crusade costs, and bring a team of 70 well -prepared prayer warriors with us. Each morning, we trained the team then sent them into the streets, market and hospital. Everyone in Port Vila recognised the people with the blue tee shirts ministering the power of the Holy Spirit to a hurting people. The meetings were amazing, with around 25% of the city attending the last meeting. The whole city was so shaken that we agreed to come back. Our return was three weeks ago, (from the time of writing), with a team of 100 fired up Christians ready to shake a city. On the final night, in a city of 46,000, nearly 20,000 attended. Our team saw a huge release of healing power. One team member saw 30 deaf people healed in the five days. One team member prayed for a lady whose baby had died in the womb. After prayer, the babe was kicking and very much alive. Watching the team working at the altar, passionate to see the sick healed and souls saved is perhaps the greatest thrill of our 40 years of ministry.

ACROSS THE WORLD

These are a sample of some of the places where we have preached over the years. What a huge privilege it has been to bring this great signs following message to Japan, Malaysia, Singapore, Uruguay, Venezuela, Estonia, Russia, Thailand, USA, UK, India, Pakistan, Myanmar, Sweden, Germany, France Holland, NZ, Indonesia, Australia and many other nations. It's just the beginning however. The opportunities opening to us are huge. The future is as big as we can dream.

"Now unto Him that is able to do exceeding abundantly above all that we ask or think, according to the power that worketh in us" (Ephesians 3:20).

CHAPTER NINE

MIRACLES

"And with great power the apostles gave witness to the resurrection of the Lord Jesus. And great grace was upon them all" - Acts 4:33 KJV

Miracles bear witness to Christ's resurrection and give authenticity to the message we preach. They draw people like insects to a light. In the Scriptures one miracle, act of power, or precise word of knowledge saw whole cities turn to Christ. In the Book of Acts, we have the one example of a New Testament evangelist in action. This was Philip. In Samaria the mighty manifestations of God's power saw multitudes flock to hear the message (see Acts 8). We have always been incredibly passionate to see powerful God encounters whenever we preach. I thought about some of the exciting miracles we have seen in the past 40 years and thought you might enjoy sharing some of these thrilling events.

CANCER AND A DEAD CHILD RAISED – PAPUA NEW GUINEA

The man's face was ashen grey. Curled up in the fetal position, they carried him into the auditorium on a military green canvas.

I was preaching a message on faith in action when I watched him carried in by several men, and laid to my right about 20 feet from the pulpit. The shadow of death seemed to hang over him like a cloud. I later discovered that cancer had started in his feet and had spread through his body. He had been bed ridden and virtually paralyzed for months. This day in Port Moresby something extraordinary was about to happen. It's always exciting watching God step in when all of man's abilities are at an end. This man was beyond hope. The same was said of Abraham that, with any reason for hope gone, he actually believed in hope that he, as an old man with an old wife with a dead womb, might become the father of many nations (see Romans 4:16-21). This situation reminded me so much of the man carried by his friends on to the rooftop and lowered to the feet of Jesus (see Mark 2:1-12).

I had preached on faith in action and now, after prayer, challenged the crowd to act on their faith and do something they couldn't previously do. God began healing people across the auditorium. I glanced to my right and noticed the man making some movements of his limbs. Two men then began pumping his legs back and forth, and my first reaction was a fear that this poor fellow would die from his friends' enthusiasm. I looked away to watch the exciting activity that filled the room. So many people were being healed. I wasn't keen to watch the poor man's body being pushed and pulled. Suddenly, gasps of excitement and pointing caused me to turn and see the man standing. He was wobbling like a new born colt, but standing. Under his feet were huge growths that made it extremely difficult to walk, yet he was taking daring steps. Faith that is acted upon is such an amazing thing. It brings pleasure to God. It was shared faith here, like the man lowered through the roof. The Scripture says, "seeing their faith," He said, "stand up and walk." These men, seeing him starting to move, had grown in faith and had begun working with him. They had already carried him some distance in expectation of this moment. Jesus had seen their faith. Now the man was taking shaky steps forward.

Without thinking about it, but more by sheer instinct, both Jacque and I pointed and shouted to those great tumours to go. Instantly his feet were flat on the floor. He took off walking, then jogging, which was something that had not happened for many months. This was normal Christianity in the Book of Acts and this should be expected today. That night we were ministering at the National Stadium. Sadly, heavy rain hit with a vengeance that day, which badly affected the size of the crowd. Instead of tens of thousands of people in the stadium, there were perhaps about 5000 people sheltering under large colourful umbrellas. Among them, we were told, was our friend who had been miraculously healed. He was found and brought up onto the stage. Truly he looked like an Olympic athlete, fit and vital. He jogged about, demonstrating the awesome work that Jesus had performed. That wet, soaking night, an even greater miracle would take place.

As the tropical deluge of rain began pouring down, many in our already depleted crowd scattered. Two feet of water began flooding under the platform and the sound system began sparking dangerously. With all the cables and electrics on the platform in puddles of water, it was time to for the musicians and team to abandon ship. It felt a bit like the Titanic. We were wading out through shin deep water wondering what would happen next. Well, Papua New Guineans are tough people. They were wading through the water for prayer. The power of God was coming upon them and many were falling prostrate down into the water as the anointing of healing came upon them. They were then standing up wet and dramatically healed. In the midst of this crazy and invigorating time a lady handed a baby into the arms of my friend Buck, who was one of our team from New Zealand. The little child had tubes up its nose, was blue grey in colour, and had been dead for some time. As Buck prayed, standing shin deep in water, the little one came alive from the dead. The family rejoiced and wept as the Kingdom of God came so mightily into their tragic scene. What a mighty and unchanging God we serve. As we drove back to the hotel, through flooding, muddy waters, and drenched, thrilled people, we rejoiced at the goodness of God on this wet crazy night.

DEAD CHILD RAISED – AUSTRALIA

Seeing the dead raised is quite remarkable. I recall many years ago preaching at a place called Kurri Kurri in New South Wales, Australia. Our family had been holidaying in Queensland and we were driving back to Victoria. I had committed to preach at a close friend's church on the way back. I had driven for eight hours that day and was fairly tired. My preaching that night was a struggle as I was quite drained. We were in a large public hall with a healthy mid-week crowd. I remember my preaching felt laborious that night, and the crowd seemed very restless. I was preparing to finish when I heard a lady shouting and crying as she ran up to the pulpit. She pushed a little toddler into my arms. One moment I was preaching, the next, I was holding a little child. Then the awareness seized me. The child was dead. I was standing before a confused congregation, holding a lifeless child, with a helpless despairing mother alongside me. What do you do? The mind races. All that went through my mind was, "Shout; get the people to shout." At the walls of Jericho, as Joshua and the people shouted, the walls came tumbling down (see Joshua 6). There is something tremendous that accompanies a mighty faith building shout unto the great Healer and King. Shout we did! It was purposeful and passionate and full of the declaration of God's might. I don't know whose faith caused the Hand of God to overshadow that dear little mite, but I had the enormous thrill of feeling and seeing life pour back into the child I was holding. How amazing it was to see dead eyes become filled with life. Yes, Jesus is "the same yesterday, today and forever" (see Hebrews 13:8). I was told the child had had a seizure and paramedics had tried in vain to revive the little one. I guess the child could now be thirty years of age, and likely married with a family. I doubt that I will ever know. But that moment, as a young preacher, is indelibly etched in my memory.

MIRACLES – INDIA

How Jacque and I love seeing the miracles. Over the years we have seen literally thousands of them. I recall a two-week period in India when every deaf or mute person we prayed for was healed. We've watched Jesus heal cripples, straighten limbs, and restore sight all over the world. He has promised to confirm His Word with signs and miracles following (see Mark 16:20).

"SHOCK ME" – SOUTH AFRICA

We were ministering in South Africa, which is one of our favourite places to preach. We have been going there now for many years. I was awakened on a Sunday morning by a powerful sense of God's anointing. He spoke to me very clearly this way: "Tim, I want you to ask me something." "What should I ask?" I replied. He said, "Ask me to shock you." I replied, "Lord, please shock me today!" That morning meeting was powerful. The Lord was moving with great healings, but I wasn't shocked. I was looking for the extraordinary. That night, as I recall, I preached on expectation. Souls were saved and miracles of healing began to occur. Suddenly, at the back of the auditorium, there was a big commotion. A lady and her daughter of around twelve-years-old were both sobbing as they were brought to the front. "What happened?" I asked the lady. Through her sobs, she explained that her daughter had been born with a withered leg. The thigh of one leg was about half the diameter of the other. She could never play sport or live like a normal young girl. As we prayed, the lady declared they had felt the engulfing power of God. As the girl shook under the creative Hand of God, her leg began vibrating. Her mother lifted her skirt to see the leg growing to the same size as the other. I was shocked and thrilled but taken aback, as I felt the Lord's mild and caring rebuke: "I don't want you to be shocked by this! I want you to expect this as normal." Truly this type of miracle should be what we expect. God is wanting to do "exceedingly abundantly beyond anything we can ask think or imagine" (see Ephesians 3:20).

Many people say to us cynically that we only see the great miracles in the developing nations. This is so untrue. Some of the most wonderful things we have seen have been in the First World. My wife Jacquelyn carries a powerful healing anointing. In the Philippines she watched an eye form in a lady's empty socket, which was thrilling. However, here in Australia, New Zealand, England and America we have been equally inspired and amazed.

STROKE – AUSTRALIA

Recently Jacque prayed for a lady here in Melbourne, Australia who had been terribly afflicted by a stroke. I will let Jacque tell you the story:

"At the end of my session at 'Beautiful Woman' (Planetshakers women's conference) in Melbourne, Victoria, I heard the Holy Spirit say to me, "There are people here who are grieving. Call them forward and I will set them free." It was not until later that I heard from this woman who came to tell me of the great thing that God had done for her. She had come to Melbourne to say goodbye to her father who was dying in the hospital. However, she did not know how she could do this. Three years previously she'd had a stroke that had left her without her speech and paralysed down one side. But God is still a miracle-working God. She told one of the leaders that God's power had come all over her as she responded to the 'word' that God had said about grieving in spirit. At first, she felt her limbs could move, and then she felt she could speak. So powerful was this miracle for her that she went immediately to the hospital to say goodbye to her father. She had thrown away her walker and could speak perfectly. She wept as she spoke her parting words to her dear father."

BARRENNESS

Jacque has been used often to pray for women who had been unable to have children. We constantly receive photos and testimonies of people who have been childless, often for years, who have conceived and had a child within a year of her prayer. She inspires me as she tells me of the amazing things that she saw in India and the Philippines.

AUTISM – AUSTRALIA

One night in Sydney, Australia, we saw a very inspiring miracle that had far reaching impact. A miracle should not just impact one person's life but spread through whole communities and cities. This was certainly the biblical pattern. A dear lady brought a child who was about five-years-old to one of our meetings. I believe the lady may have been a relative. She came expecting a miracle for this small autistic boy. Autism is a condition that sadly impacts a child's motor skills, emotional reactions and other areas of life. It often makes life for the parents extremely difficult. As we prayed for the sick that night, the young boy and the lady came up onto the platform. I vaguely remember praying for the boy and seeing him lying on the floor being powerfully touched by God. The lady took the boy home to his mother after the meeting. The mother had that day bought a puppy to try to touch the boy's emotions. On seeing the puppy, he ran embraced it with an excitement and emotional outburst that they had never seen before. The mother began weeping, knowing that a miracle had taken place, and began asking what had happened that night. He explained that he had seen a man that evening. Not the preacher, but the 'Great Man' – Jesus. She became afraid. "What did He say?" she blurted out. The little boy's answer sent a chill through her: "He said you are coming to Him." "Am I going to die?" she plaintively asked. "No, you are coming to Him!" She gave her life back to Jesus in that moment. The backslidden father later walked into this holy scene. From memory, the boy's sickness had been a part of the reason for him walking away previously. Overwhelmed by the scene, he was restored in his relationship to Christ. From all reports, the impact of this miracle spread through many family members.

TYPHOID - PAKISTAN

So often, as we minister in campaign meetings, we see some rather amusing things. I recall one night in Pakistan seeing a man in the crowd who appeared to be attached to a television aerial. When he came to the front, I could see that he had the hospital stand with a drip bag into his arm. He was in hospital with typhoid fever. Sweat was pouring down his face. After prayer, we watched him wander off with the drip stand. The following night, he was back, healed and discharged.

BLINDNESS

When the blind are healed we move about and ask them to touch our nose. I watched Reinhard Bonnke doing this and love to imitate his technique. Little ladies chase you about, excited by their miracle and thoroughly enjoying the chance the catch the preacher by his nose. The crowd certainly get caught up in the fun but you can sense the faith rising to great heights.

CRIPPLED MAN – NEW ZEALAND

I was preaching in Hastings and Napier, Hawke's Bay in New Zealand. It was our first night and I was nervous. The congregation numbered about 60 or 70 people. I had on my red tie and carried my black brief case that held my Bible and notes. They say an expert is someone 20 miles from home carrying a briefcase. I've also heard that an expert is a drip under pressure. I looked the part of the evangelist, had the right terminology, but was far from feeling supremely confident. I was just desperately dependent on God coming to confirm the Word.

That dependence should never fade. I think, as the years go by, and the Lord has come in power again and again, never leaving you out on a limb, but graciously demonstrating His power, we become more and more confident in His utter faithfulness.

I preached my sermon as passionately and purposefully as possible then called for souls to come to Jesus. A few people strolled down to the front to be saved and then I began ministering healing. Trying to minister healing would be more accurate. Absolutely nothing was happening. I was feeling totally spiritually impotent and helpless. It was me trying to make something happen. It's a terrible position to be in! I worked my way down the healing line, shouting and spitting, with no sign of God's power. I felt like getting on the next plane out and never going after miracles again. At times, in those early days, I would get so discouraged when little crippled children weren't healed. I used to feel haunted by the despairing looks in their desperate parents' eyes. In those days, I would often go home feeling that I was a fraud as so few were healed. We saw a few good things happen that kept us hungry. I'm so glad I didn't throw in the towel. There is a passion to keep pushing on, believing for breakthrough! That passion to keep believing builds something deep within. The quest to work with God in total dependence, shaking off all our doubts, is so vital in our growth. I've learned not to be dejected by what doesn't happen in meetings but to be incredibly thankful to God for what does happen. I used to remind myself that Jesus Himself, carrying the Spirit without measure, could only heal a few sick people in his home town of Nazareth. He marvelled at their unbelief (see Mark 6:1-6). I began to fervently pray that God would give me His key messages that would stimulate faith for the impossible. At the end of this line, I was feeling totally desperate when suddenly the anointing of God hit the last man with a surge of healing grace that sent him crashing to the floor. My eyes bugged out of my head in amazement.

Up he jumped, miraculously healed of a painful back condition. It seemed he was the only one touched that night, but he had been totally healed by a burst of God's lightning fire.

That night I sat in the pastor's home knowing that, apart from one thing, the meeting had been dismal. We finished up laughing together at my poor showing as an evangelist and realized that tomorrow would be a new day of opportunities.

The day started with a jolt. It was the healed guy on the phone at 7.00 am. "How can you phone the evangelist at that hour?" I thought. He was so positive about the miracle he had received. I was starting to feel quite positive in faith, and ready to face night two. "This is great," I thought, just before he dropped the bombshell. It went something like this: "I'm so excited that I phoned my crippled friend and told him you would come over at 10.00 am to raise him up." I thought, "Crippled! What am I facing?" I wondered why he couldn't have just enjoyed his miracle instead of throwing me into what seemed like the lion's den. Then I wished I hadn't asked the question about his crippled friend's situation. It went like this: "My friend was crushed against a wall by a truck, crushing his spine. He is bent over double, having constant painkillers for the absolute agony he suffers. His spine is twisted, so that one of his legs is much shorter than the other. He's not a Christian but I told him you carry the healing gift from Jesus." Catching the next plane home seemed so inviting. I felt trapped and terrified. I had seen a paralysed arm healed, but this was far more serious. I was looking deeper and deeper into my fears and insecurities.

The drive to the house was torment. I was in a cold sweat and just wanted to run. I've learnt over the years to never run from but towards the challenge. David taught us that, as he sprinted towards

Goliath with his sling in hand. We rang the doorbell and waited. The man's wife met us, with the words, "Thanks for coming, but he is much worse today. Could you go and sit in the living room?" Where would I start? What words should I use? I could hear their voices and could hear him shuffling slowly up the passage from his room. One glance at this broken, pale, pain-wracked shell of a man sent any slight semblance of faith in me scattering to the four winds. As he struggled down into an arm chair, emitting sounds and pain-filled utterances, I didn't want to look his way. This was out of my hands. It was beyond any human or psychological method that could be brought into play. I'm sure many sicknesses are psychosomatic but this was certainly not. This was a smashed spine, which the most skilled surgeons could not fix. Only God Himself could do this.

"I can't heal you Lee," I blurted out, "but Jesus can." This is not strictly scriptural. Jesus has given us His name and His power and the instruction for us to go and heal in His name. I was throwing this totally back in Jesus' court. Without looking at Lee, I began reading the Scriptures on healing from Exodus, through the Psalms, Isaiah, then on into the New Testament Gospels. I don't think I looked at him once in all the reading. Suddenly, I felt compelled to look up. I saw this amazed, incredibly expectant, look in his eyes and on his face. "He's about to get healed," I thought. I knew it. The room was filled with expectancy and the electric sense of God. I called the pastor and the man who was healed on the last night. As I walked towards Lee, I felt as bold as a lion. This was how the apostles must have felt at the Gate Beautiful (see Acts 3). I knew, as certainly as anything I could know, that something remarkable was about to take place before our eyes. I took Lee by the hands and, just like the Bible stories, commanded him to stand up straight. He struggled up to his feet. I then commanded, "Stand up straight! Do it now!" There was a cracking of this crushed spine, as the restoring might of our Saviour went through him. Up he stood, straight and tall. Tears flowed all through that small crowd. A profound miracle had occurred before our eyes. "It's not by might nor by power," rang in my mind (see Zechariah 4:6). This was not a work of man's ability. How could any person claim the glory for this? This was the resurrected Son of God, moving through us and with us. If God could do that through nervous, intimidated, almost reluctant believers, what can He do when we boldly stand in total dependence on him in stadiums, football fields, schools, universities, and churches across the globe? That day was a major step for me in the area of total dependence on Him. The meetings there grew to many hundreds and many great healings occurred. Don't ever let a day of seeming failure crush you or discourage you. Grit your teeth, hold fast to God, and go into the next phase in the program He has for you. Always keep in mind that King Jesus is with you, in you, and through you to confirm His Word with a great demonstration of power.

"And they went forth, and preached everywhere, the Lord working with [them], and confirming the word with signs following. Amen" (Mark 16:20).

TEAMS – MIRACLES

Our great passion now is training teams of people of all ages to move in the gifts of the Spirit in a most powerful way. Over the past few years, we have stepped up the size of the teams we have been taking with us on our international campaigns. The number of miracles we see are multiplying with every campaign. For a number of years, we took only our team and a group of preachers. These were successful but I knew we could achieve much more with a clear plan. The real revelation of the impact of anointed teams came in Papua New Guinea with the group from Popondetta, as I discussed in the previous chapter. Watching this team, who has fasted and prayed in preparation for the crusade, and their passion to pray for the sick was inspiring. When we released them into the crowd, miracles broke out on every side. I watched as people began to scream and fall as the team continued to press into the expectant crowd. I knew from that night, that this was God's plan for the future.

We began taking teams of 15 to 20 people along to each campaign. They were a cross-section of folk of all ages and backgrounds. Each morning, we would teach principles of healing and miracles, pray, then send the team into the markets and streets to preach, share, and see miracles occur.

Seeing miracles breaking out in the markets did several things. Firstly, the people would be aware of the night rallies and be inspired to attend. They would also become confident that the team were as capable of getting the miracles as the evangelist. This made my work at night so much easier but also multiplied the results greatly. Over the last few years, teams have become as large as 100 people. They all wear a bright coloured distinguishing T-shirt as they preach and pray through the markets, schools, hospitals, and jails. On several occasions, as many as 80% of the hospital patients have been released on the day our teams have gone through. On a recent five-day crusade in Vanuatu, one team member (who works as a builder) saw over 30 deaf people healed. Others saw amazing miracles, including a baby, who was dead in the womb restored to life, cripples, blind people, stroke victims, cancers and tumours healed. Our real joy is seeing the thrill and excitement on the faces of our team members as we sit together discussing events of the meetings. They always return home inspired, changed, and aware of what God has put in their lives.

CHAPTER TEN

MENTORS

"Mentoring is a brain to pick, an ear to listen and a push in the right direction" – **John C Crosby**

I love the questions that my Bible students ask at Planetshakers College. One question that often gets asked is, "Who are your mentors and who inspires you?" We all have our favourite preachers and visionaries whose exploits, daring and powerful grip of God's Word have inspired us. We will never meet many of them, yet we feel we know them like family. We listen to their preaching and read their books. We long to imitate their deeds.

When I was first saved, I listened to every tape I could lay my hands on by Oral Roberts, the great American preacher. His simple, yet potent, preaching carried an authority that was tangible. Even the resonance of his voice seemed alive with a holy voltage of power. He knew who he was! He knew what he carried from the Lord. There was a weight to his words. Jesus said, in John 6:63: "The words that I speak to you, they are Spirit and they are Life." So many preachers have great sermons and are exciting communicators, but there is not that deep, power-laden sense of certainty and spiritual authority in their words. This authority seems to fill the words of the daring, hungry people of prayer.

I remember God speaking to me as a young man: " Tim, what do you want to be?" My answer was simple, "I want to be a preacher." I felt a pause, then these words resonated through my spirit: "I have plenty of preachers. I am searching for men and women of God, people who are carriers of my Kingdom power."

The great miracle move of God in the 1950's, with people like T.L. and Daisy Osborne, F.F. Bosworth, A.A. Allen and so many others, fascinated me. I still watch A.A. Allen on You Tube clips and marvel at his bold faith. Smith Wigglesworth's writings have always stirred me to strive for a greater capacity to release all that God has given us to minister. Possibly the preacher who has stirred me most by his writings is John G. Lake. His daring 'adventures in God' always send a thrill through my soul.

The wonderful ladies Katherine Kuhlman and Maria Woodworth-Etter moved in dimensions of Holy Ghost power that have been unique. My first pastor and father in the faith, Dr Andrew Evans, who incidentally has been a huge mentor to me, described a Katherine Kuhlman meeting in this way. I had watched her on VHS. She was very dramatic and theatrical, yet amazingly sensitive, giving all glory to her Jesus. Pastor Evans described the moment that the great auditorium became impregnated with a holy awe. "I feel the great presence of the Holy Spirit," she declared, in a calculated way that carried a sense of total awe, as miracles began to break out all over the auditorium like a torrent of heavenly rain. She began, by the word of knowledge, to point to different sections of the awestruck crowd calling conditions, nationalities and the sudden miracles like the conductor of a great orchestra. My pastor wrote page after page of amazing healings until he could no longer write because of his own tears that began to flood the page.

Over 40 years of ministry, it has been a great thrill to form a relationship with many amazing servants of God. Spending time with Evangelist Reinhard Bonnke has been a great highlight in my life. So few men have ever seen souls saved like this man. Sitting with him, at lunch in Brisbane, Australia, I asked if there was some word of inspiration he could share with me regarding global evangelism. I watched with interest his face, which is so well known to vast multitudes of humanity. His eyes seemed to intensify like a laser. I could almost see in them the 50 million souls that had been won in the previous decade through this giant, whose name is now etched in the history of the people of faith. "Souls, souls and after that more souls," he said. I knew I was looking into the face of a man totally sold out to winning vast, uncountable multitudes of humanity. As a young man, stepping out in ministry, I placed on my wall big posters of the great crowds attending his campaigns. I dreamed and prayed that one day this would be my destiny.

In our own country, some great ministries have been mentors and mighty inspirations. Dr Andrew Evans was my first pastor who took me under his wing from day one. He built into me a great sense of confidence, self-belief, and released me into ministry. As his youth pastor, he encouraged me continually and watered the great hunger that God had given me for His power. I knew, despite my rawness and at times scattered approach, he believed in me and constantly built confidence in me. We saw a wonderful revival among our youth. He would, at times, take me with him as he spoke at conferences and camp meetings. He would release me to pray for people at the altar, recognising the anointing that I carried for this area of ministry. To this day, he treats me as one of his sons in ministry.

Today we are based with Andrew's son Russell and his wife Samantha. Their mighty gifting has seen Planetshakers church grow from zero to 12 thousand people in 10 years. Their single-minded passion is a continual inspiration. Pastor Russell has an uncanny ability to hear from God and act on it without delay. He constantly dreams big and dares to step out with great results.

Pastors Brian and Bobbie Houston of Hillsong have inspired me with their unstoppable sense of passion to seize ground for God, and they continually move forward on a huge scale. Their global impact is nothing short of a phenomenon.

Pastor Phil Pringle of Christian City Churches has been a significant person to spend time with. He, too, is a huge thinker with a huge global dream. The scale of their visions inspire and thrill me. We must surround ourselves with people who stretch and challenge us to achieve huge things. Preaching in these great churches is always soul stirring. In South Africa, my friends Pastor At Boshoff and Pastor Ray McCauley always cause me to dream bigger. Both men have been used of God globally, and in South Africa to see hundreds of thousands of people established in the Kingdom. Dr Rodney Howard-Browne of Tampa, Florida came along side me at a time of incredible personal pain. The mighty anointing that he carries helped me into a place of emotional restoration during the toughest time of my life. That sense of anointing and his ability and passion to impart the power of God has greatly inspired my life. These people are giants.

Apart from Jesus, the apostle Paul is my greatest Biblical mentor. As a baby, I was christened Gordon Stewart Hall. Six weeks later, I was to see my grandfather Thomas Hall, who was called Tim by everyone. For some reason, my mother and grandmother decided that they would call me Tim after Thomas even though I was Gordon. That certainly was confusing. I added the name Timothy by deed poll, at a cost of two dollars, when I was 27-years-old. It seemed logical at the time, but now I'm convinced it is my God-given name. I love dearly Paul's epistles to young Timothy, the pastor of the church at Ephesus.

To a young man, Paul wrote, "Be an imitator of me as I am of Christ" (1 Corinthians 11:1). Paul was more than a preacher or a great apostle. He was a gladiatorial warrior in the great arena of faith. He approached the work of ministry with a sense of desperate, fearless purpose. His ministry was a ministry of demonstration of power and amazing miracles.

"Through mighty signs and wonders, by the power of the Spirit of God; so that from Jerusalem, and round about unto Illyricum, I have fully preached the gospel of Christ" (Romans 15:19).

His final days are always a huge challenge to finish the race strongly.

Paul the great apostle, sat in the infamous Maritime Prison in Rome knowing that at any time Praetorian guards would drag him out of that cold stinking place to die a violent and cruel death. Emperor Nero's savaging of Christians was barbaric and merciless. Murder was, to his deranged mind, an art form. Paul was his prize prey, and time was fast drawing to a close for the old gladiator of Christ whose fearless, selfless onslaught had changed the world in a way that no great general in history had done. Certainly, Alexander of Macedonia had Hellenised the world, bringing mighty change. Gaius Julius Caesar's conquest of the Gauls had extended Rome's territory to the English Channel and the Rhine. So many great generals have come and gone shaping our world but none, save King Jesus Himself, have left the impact on history that Paul, the great general of faith, has left.

Paul certainly didn't preach a diluted gospel. He preached with a certain understanding that death stared him in the face each time he stood up to speak. His response was to look death squarely in the eye, and then fully preach the Gospel of the Kingdom with mighty signs, wonders and miracles confirming the Word. It is obviously possible to water down the preaching of God's Word to make it more palatable, but this was never Paul's approach. He preached as one contesting for men's souls in a savage cauldron of hostility. Paul's full frontal, fearless preaching flooded a community with an undeniable manifestation of the raw, undisputed power of a supernatural God who had come with great purpose. Cities of the Ancient world shook as he stepped onto their centre stage, carrying the overwhelming power and presence of the One he had once so violently persecuted.

Now he sat alone in this cold cell, breathing the acrid stench that seemed to permeate the very walls of this place of terror. The screams and plaintive cries of men, facing torture and death without hope, filled the air. The cold heavy chains held him to the dark stone walls. For most, despair and terror would flood their sleepless final days. Paul had been abandoned by nearly everyone whose souls he had nurtured. All in Asia had left him. Only faithful Luke was coming to him. Yet Paul was buoyant, alive in spirit, and amazingly positive. From this place of death and horror, he wrote exhilarating words of strength and certainty to a frightened young pastor at Ephesus. The second epistle to young Timothy is filled with dynamic certainty and a soul-stirring challenge to stand strong, resolute and certain in the face of anything Satan can bring against you: "For God hath not given us the spirit of fear; but of power, and of love, and of a sound mind" (2 Timothy 1:7).

Paul seemed to fear nothing in his quest to spread the undiluted Gospel across the nations.

Paul's life set up for me a blue print for world evangelism. After Jesus, his life covers the characteristics that inspire me the most. In closing this chapter, one thought fills my mind. Am I living a life that will cause people to see me as someone with characteristics and passion that would cause me in some way to be a mentor to them? How can we inspire this next generation? I really believe that our success will be judged more by the impact we leave on the next generation than what we have done ourselves. Let's leave a foundation upon which they can build.

CHAPTER ELEVEN

THE FUTURE

**"The future is as bright as the promises of God"
– William Carey**

I was recently asked if we were considering retirement sometime soon. I felt taken back and almost offended. I wondered why we would consider this. What would we do? Perhaps we could buy rocking chairs, get a cat, and spend the day watching the History Channel on Foxtel. I could go down to the shop each morning and buy the paper, then complete the Sudoku while drinking a nice hot Cappuccino. We could also grow tomatoes, which would be difficult living in an apartment in the Docklands of Melbourne.

No, retirement isn't something we are contemplating. In fact, the challenge is now to dream and plan bigger than ever before. Caleb, the Bible hero, started his greatest days after his 85th birthday. He began to seize his inheritance as a very old man, yet Scripture tells us that he was as strong at 85 as he had been at 40.

"As yet I am as strong this day as I was in the day that Moses sent me: as my strength was then, even so is my strength now, for war, both to go out, and to come in" (Joshua 14:11).

No, we feel that the first 40 years have been merely the training school and preparation time.

As we study God's Word, the number 40 becomes very significant. It is used 146 times. It can speak of a generation, but generally it is seen as a time of testing, trial or probation. Rain fell on the earth for 40 days and 40 nights in Noah's day. The children of Israel wandered the Sinai Peninsula for 40 years before their entrance to the promised land. Twice, Moses went up onto mount Sinai at the command of the Lord. Each time it was for a period of 40 days. 40 spies were sent into the promised land. Jonah preached repentance in Nineveh for 40 days and Elijah fasted 40 days on Mount Horeb. Jesus went into the wilderness to fast and pray for 40 days, during which he was tested by the devil.

The last 40 years of ministry were a time of probation, learning, experience, and testing of the devil, but coming through this has brought us to our most significant and fruitful time. What do we do now? Our first goal is to impact whole nations with the greatest impact we have ever seen. In a world full of chaos and uncertainty, it is time for bold, fearless Christians to stand up, clothed in a mighty dimension of power and grace. It is also a time to impart everything we have learned into the next generation.

I have often read the remarkable miracle in 2 Kings 13 of the dead man who was raised by Elisha's bones. On the arrival of Midianite marauders, a funeral procession scattered, leaving only the men carrying the dead man in an open coffin. Rather than just leave the body, they dropped it into the tomb of Elisha. Amazingly, there was still enough of God's power in the prophet's bones to raise a man from the dead. I would marvel at this great miracle, until one day I heard God whisper in my ear, "What was that great anointing doing in a dead man's tomb?" Elijah imparted his mantle to Elisha. Jesus left the mighty Holy Spirit with us. Paul took people with him on missionary trips and longed to come and impart spiritual gifts to those he was raising up. How sad is it that so many men of God go to their grave without raising up the next generation to carry the baton? David raised up mighty men who, like himself, became significant giant killers. Our aim from here is not only to conduct great campaign meetings globally, but to train up hundreds, even thousands, of fired up and powerfully equipped, nation-seizing ministries. We believe that success in ministry should be judged, not so much on what we achieve, but on who we have raised up to follow us. Elijah left a prophet with a double portion of his gift while Elisha took his gifting to the grave. I personally want to follow the Elijah model.

The first 40 years have been absolutely amazing. Now it is time to take on the next decade. The future is as big as we can dream! Paul lets us know what God can do:

"Now to him who is able to do immeasurably more than all we ask or imagine, according to his power that is at work within us, to him be glory in the church and in Christ Jesus throughout all generations, for ever and ever! Amen" (Ephesians 3:20-21).

ENDNOTES

Chapter One

1 Bendigo Historical Society, 2016, 'Discovery of Gold', http://www.bendigohistory.com/discovery_of_gold.shtml , accessed 26 September 2016.

2 *Australian Town and Country Journal*, 21 September 1878,

http://trove.nla.gov.au/newspaper/article/70595069 , accessed 26 September 2016.

3 "Evangelist (Bendigo)",2016, http://myweb.tiscali.co.uk/sherwoodtimes/evangeli.htm , accessed 28 September 2016.

4 Studeny, Richard, 13 November 2014, 'Nottinghamshire Legends: Bendigo', http://www.bbc.co.uk/nottingham/content/articles/2005/02/14/features_people_2005_02_bendigo_and_forest_tavern_feature.shtml , accessed 28 September 2016.

Chapter Two

5 'Is God Dead?', https://en.wikipedia.org/wiki/Is_God_Dead-%3F , accessed 27 September 2016.

Chapter Seven

6 King Jr., Martin Luther, 1960, http://literarydevices.net/if-you-cant-fly-then-run/ , accessed 10 October 2016.

7 Churchill, Winston S., 2004, *Never Give In! The Best of Winston Churchill's Speeches,* https://www.goodreads.com/work/quotes/26316-never-give-in-the-best-of-winston-churchill-s-speeches , accessed 10 October 2016.

8 Churchill, Winston, https://www.goodreads.com/author/quotes/2834066.Winston_Churchill , accessed 10 October 2016.

9 https://en.wikipedia.org/wiki/Coober_Pedy , accessed 10 October 2016.

10 Churchill, Winston, https://www.goodreads.com/author/quotes/2834066.Winston_Churchill , accessed 10 October 2016.

Chapter Eight

11https://www.google.com.au/destination?dest_mid=/m/04vmp&sa=X&ved=0ahUKEwjYgvvkttLPAhXLGT-4KHaoAApEQri4ImQEwFw , accessed 11 October 2016.

ABOUT THE AUTHOR

Tim Hall is an Australian evangelist who has ministered extensively in churches and great outdoor crusades across the nations for over 40 years. He and his wife Jacquelyn reside in Melbourne. They are actively involved in ministry at Planetshakers church, led by Pastors Russell and Samantha Evans, where Tim is part of the Eldership. Between Tim and Jacquelyn, they have five children and ten grandchildren. Their ministry Tim Hall International Ministries Incorporated has seen over one million souls saved and huge numbers healed. After 40 successful years of ministry, Tim's words are: "We are just getting started."

Clockwise from top left: Timothy Gordon Stewart Hall - Born 16/12/1948; Jacquelyn Hall preaching; We love our ten grandchildren; Deborah, Ashleigh, Dave

Papua New Guinea
1992

Left: Papua New
Guinea 2016;
Below left: Broken
arm healed in
PNG; Below right:
Crippled man
healed PNG

Above: Gujarat, India; Below: Neyvelli, India

Security men - Lahore, Pakistan

Left: Karachi, Pakistan; Below: CLC Church - Bloemfontein, South Africa

Top: Former Communist Cultural Center - Tallin, Estonia 1991;

Middle: Cripple man healed - Port Villa, Vanuatu 2016;

Below: Ministry in the United States

Above: Bogota, Colombia - 2016
Below left: Miracles in Florida , USA - 2014;
Below right: Jacque ministering healing - Port Vila, Vanuatu 2016

Above: Myanmar (Burma)

Below: Port Vila, Vanuatu - 2016

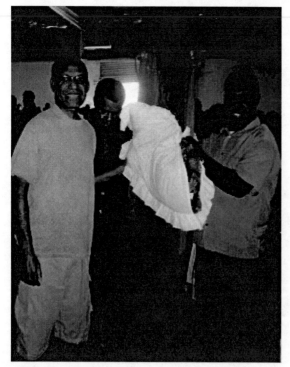

Above: Myanmar
(Burma) - 2014

Left: Extra ordinary
miracle, PNG

CPSIA information can be obtained
at www.ICGtesting.com
Printed in the USA
FSOW01n1928270417
33476FS